THE RETURN
OF
ARTHUR CONAN DOYLE

THE RETURN
OF
ARTHUR CONAN DOYLE

Edited by IVAN COOKE

THE WHITE EAGLE PUBLISHING TRUST
LISS · HAMPSHIRE · ENGLAND

MCMLXXXV

First published as THY KINGDOM COME
(*Wright & Brown, London*), DECEMBER 1933
Second edition, December 1935
THE RETURN OF ARTHUR CONAN DOYLE,
substantially revised, published 1956 (issued February 1957)
Second edition, October 1963
Third edition, June 1975 (paper bound)
Fourth edition, April 1980
Reprinted, March 1985

© *Copyright, in the present revised edition,*
The White Eagle Publishing Trust, 1963, 1975

British Library Cataloguing in Publication Data

The return of Arthur Conan Doyle. – 4th ed.
1. Spiritualism
I. Doyle, *Sir* Arthur Conan   II. Cooke, Grace
III. Cooke, Ivan
133.9′3   BF1343

ISBN 0–85487–045–8

Set in 12 on 13pt Bembo
Printed in Great Britain by
FLETCHER AND SON LIMITED, NORWICH

CONTENTS

ILLUSTRATIONS

PREFACE

SINCE it is said that nobody reads a preface, this need only be brief. Sir Arthur Conan Doyle was—as the world knows—an ardent Spiritualist. After his death in 1930, however, he discovered that many of the Spiritualist beliefs which he himself had sponsored needed revision in the light of his own experience. Being a man of forthright honesty and sincerity, heaven itself could not hold him until he had made his truth known. His family, convinced from the outset that it was he himself who had come back, helped him throughout. This book contains the new revelation of Spiritualism that he made.

His message, however, far exceeded the bounds of Spiritualism; what came through was more in the nature of a religion common to all men. Nearly two years were occupied in the reception of the message; and the manuscript account was submitted to Lady Conan Doyle on its completion, who wrote to the compiler that she and her family had read ' their father's script' with great care and attention, and were ' tremendously impressed' with the result.

The message dealt with man's life after death perhaps more incisively than ever before, making clear how life here and life after death are inextricably interwoven, the one being complementary to the other. It then dealt with man's eternal progress beyond death. It answered the question of freewill versus destiny, and gave a solution to the problem of evil. It outlined a scheme for the healing of all disease. It formed, in fact, a comprehensive view of all life, its meaning and goal.

Sir Arthur's book, under the title THY KINGDOM COME, was published before the Second World War, but its length prohibited its further publication under the conditions then obtaining.

Since the demand for the book has remained constant and unsatisfied, it has now been republished in this revised edition.

The contents have been more conveniently arranged. Part I deals with the events which preceded the message. Part II is the message itself, clarified by the omission of comments and references which were necessary when the book first appeared. But Part III is new.

Since the message makes plain the *whence* of man, *why* he is here to live on earth, and *whither* he goes after death, it is not too much to say that it forms a common basis of universal religion, and thus merits careful reading; after which it will remain for the reader to decide how far these statements justify themselves in the pages which follow.

PREFACE TO SECOND EDITION

THIS Second Edition—though properly the fourth if the two earlier editions under the title THY KINGDOM COME are included—has become necessary because of the ever-widening demand in all English-speaking countries for the ' Conan Doyle message.' Translations into Dutch and Swedish have also appeared. When giving his message, Sir Arthur said these words: ' I am under the direction of the Wise Ones. I am their servant, their instrument, and I have presently to organise this group for a future work in London. *This teaching, these messages are to be the foundation of that work.*' And again, ' I believe that He will give me the power and opportunity to carry this message to the uttermost parts of the earth.'

Since then his message has indeed reached the 'uttermost parts' of the free world, where it has been closely and deeply studied. It has been found to have its own power of persuasion, of conviction; and we feel strongly that Sir Arthur still watches over the message that he gave to the hearts of men.

PART I

THE STORY

CHAPTER I

HOW THIS BOOK CAME TO BE WRITTEN

' Of that region beyond the sky no *earthly* bard has yet sung, or ever will sing, in worthy strains.'

—Plato.

' He who waits to obtain true faith must *know;* because faith grows out of spiritual knowledge. The faith that comes from that knowledge is rooted in the heart.'

—Paracelsus.

MAN has explored his world with some thoroughness by now. Neither land nor sea nor air seem to withhold their mysteries; and he makes plans to visit the moon and planets. There seems no limit to his ambition, no secret of nature able to withstand his search for knowledge—save only one, self-knowledge; for the knowledge of his own nature, his own destiny, his *whence, why* and *whither*, is denied to all but a few. Man is still largely ignorant of the background from which he came—if any; he sees no reasonable explanation of his own existence, or clear outline of what will happen to him when his mortal span comes to an end. With these same problems students of religion, of philosophy, and in lesser degree of medicine and healing, have wrestled throughout the centuries, mostly in vain. This is why we are told by priests that man has to live by faith; that is, by an unflinching faith in what someone said many centuries ago, recorded in some book now held sacred; or else by faith in this or that interpretation of that book by some dignitary of this, that, or the other church. Such a faith is enjoined on man because, so he is told, there can be no other way of finding out anything about himself or his God.

However, some progress at least has been made, if only in the domain of faith. We have evolved systems of morality, philosophy, conduct and religion that on the whole serve the

I

community well enough. Yet one subject remains about which the average man not only knows nothing but expects to continue to know nothing, namely, his own future (and more important) the future of some loved one after death. Of all the mysteries, he believes, death is the most profound, the most unsearchable. This is perhaps why the Church has long declared that its God has purposely forbidden or debarred man from knowledge. ' " Thus far and no further," saith the Lord.' This is ironical enough; for if death terminates everything for evermore, then man's having existed at all is a baffling, futile and often tragic mystery.

Can this be true? For nothing is really worth while to us if the grave ends everything. Do we believe this? On the whole, no; we need no telling that so far as worldly wealth is concerned none of us can take it with us; but we still believe that there is an enduring yet imponderable wealth of the character, mind or spirit which might survive. To set forth why we believe this would deter most of us. We inherited our belief, perhaps, so that it has become part and parcel of our being. Because of some instinct or intuitive knowledge deep in us we hold fast to this belief that something in us can and will survive because it is *worthy to survive*. The thought of extinction at death outrages our sense of rightness, fairness and justice. We feel that any decent man deserves decent treatment from his God. To snuff him out at death is not decent treatment; but why God should have forbidden us to inquire into these matters (as the Church has declared over the centuries) is puzzling in the extreme.*

What some of us really want, and want desperately to feel sure about, is not so much our own survival but a sure hope of reunion with those dear to us who have gone before. Without this the idea of personal survival loses much of its attraction. No one wants to totter off to some ghostly location after death, there to wander alone while time drags on and on. We feel unwilling to participate in such a scheme of survival.

---

* Yet even the Anglican and Free Churches are now beginning to enquire whether it has been proved by psychic communication that man actually survives the grave—thus strengthening the need for religion.

And yet whither can we flee for definite knowledge, for assurance in these matters? Surely, someone must know—perhaps one or other of those several great Ones, on whose words and lives the sacred Scriptures of the world are based, has told us?

Astonishingly enough, it is not so. The various Scriptures contain scant promise of personal survival or of reunion with those who have gone before. At first sight this will seem too heartless to be true. The Christian will ask, what about the resurrection of Jesus? Is not this both a promise and demonstration that all of us will survive death in a like manner?

True enough; but can it be argued that what was possible for Jesus Christ, called the Son of God, is also possible not only to the Christian but to any and every man? Does this seem reasonable? The pick of the world's mountaineers can scale Everest by risk and effort. Could the man in the street? No. Neither can he climb far enough up the spiritual heights to warrant comparison with Jesus Christ. Neither do the four Gospels confirm the hope of the bereaved that they will rejoin their loved ones again in some better land. The Church burial service, it is true, is made up of texts which seem to promise such happenings, but these are culled for that special purpose from the vast body of statements which constitute the Bible; and in any case it is possible to select another array of texts which promise nothing. 'The dead know not anything' can be cited as typical of these, which can cancel out the others. Nevertheless, the hope and belief are prevalent that if there be a God of love He will surely grant this desired reunion; and there the matter rests.

Nor can it be said that the religions of the East are in much better case. They hardly mention survival (as an *isolated* fact). *Karma*, the sequence of cause and effect resulting in exact justice eventually and infallibly meted out to each soul—yes; and coupled with *Karma* comes Reincarnation, which is essential to such a plan. But we are not told what happens to the soul *between* its incarnations. Before Karma can properly work itself out, not one but many lifetimes are required. The *Bhagavad Gita* is an impressive literary masterpiece setting forth this philosophy, and in its grandeur may bear comparison with the stellar universe itself—and yet also seem as distant and un-approachable to the average man of the West.

Certainly there is little here to comfort the mourner with any promise of reunion. For in such philosophies a personal and human love is somewhat at a discount, and is cited as a form (modified perhaps) of *desire* for someone or something; and desire, we are told, is what the soul must get rid of at all costs—unless it is to remain on the ever-turning wheel of Karmic desire and therefore of recurrent incarnations. Get rid of desire, it is said in the East, and once and for all the soul is for ever freed of earth with all its sorrowful folk, and hears no more that cry of human sorrow ' which has no language but a cry.'

If there is little here to comfort the mourner, whither then must he turn for what he so desperately needs in the way of assurance and comfort in the hour of grief? Can any one of the more modern faiths assuage his sorrow? Theosophy, Christian Science, Spiritualism—what of these?

It is well known that Theosophy is largely compounded from the various religions of the East, and as such presents both Karma and Reincarnation to its devotees, but not always in an attractive or most reasonable aspect. So also with the Theo-sophical doctrine of the after-life, which appears to some chilly and unappetising. Not here will the mourner find what he needs. So also with that which Christian Science proclaims concerning the after-life, which is so seemingly contradictory that it is difficult to conceive of the average man (not a Christian Scientist) getting much help here.

This brings us to Spiritualism as a last resort. If the Churches and even their more modern variants have little to say about survival, and almost nothing about reunion beyond the grave, Spiritualism stands for almost nothing else but survival, and has as its dearest theme reunion beyond the grave.

For here alone do we find *evidence* pointing to survival, *proof* of life after death, as against conviction based on faith. There is hardly any other *evidence* of this nature forthcoming. But, no one knows, the reader will say; if that evidence is worth anything; if it were really valid and true, practically everybody would accept it right away. Instead, everybody—or rather, most sensible people—simply will not have anything to do with it. The whole thing is continually being exposed in the press, considered much too foolish to take on trust, and in the past was denounced by the Church.

Quite so; all this may be true. What everyone is saying merits respect. Yet during all the centuries of mankind man has produced nothing else capable of putting aside the sting of death. Without it, O grave, thy victory overrides every human being and wounds each loving heart! Even then, to establish survival and reunion is not enough. It does not carry us far enough. Of itself it is only one item of what we want to know. An average human life here is bitter and hard, and often seems to drag on far too long. Even when a man believes in the after-life, when he waits and even longs for it, often it seems too much like pie-in-the-sky which never comes. This is because survival by itself is by no means a complete religion. To couple this belief or surety of survival possessed by the Spiritualist with any of the orthodox religions will not solve the problem. What does then?

Only an orderly and reasonable explanation of man's being here on earth; only the purposeful setting forth of an outline or scheme which will co-relate this human life of ours with the life (or successive lives) which follows after death—only this can solve our problem of living rightly and dying hopefully and happily. The revelation of such a scheme is in fact the purpose of the present book, and this in as simple a manner as possible. Its theme falls naturally into three parts: the story of the events which brought about the revelation; the revelation itself—the scheme of man's life here and its continuation in the hereafter; and finally an evaluation of the facts narrated.

CHAPTER II

THE BOY WHO BECAME WORLD FAMOUS

' They and such as they nourish for ever that great old trunk of England, which still sheds forth another crop and another, each as strong and as fair as the last. The rumour of noble lives, the record of valour and truth can never die, but lives on in the soul of the people. Our own work lies ready to our hands; yet our strength may be the greater and our faith the firmer if we spare an hour from present toils to look back on the women who were gentle and strong, or the men who loved honour more than life on this green stage of England where for a few short years we play our little part.'

—The concluding passage of the book, *Sir Nigel*,
by Arthur Conan Doyle.

EVERY river has its tributary streams which discharge into its waters, and one or more of these can be claimed as the actual source of the river. This can also happen with a story, when several lesser stories just meander separately and then merge into the main stream. Thus, the present story might begin with the strange tale of the Hermit of Bagnaia in 1908; or with the later career of Sir Arthur Conan Doyle; or the early work of the well-known medium, authoress and seer, Mrs. Grace Cooke. The lives of all three are inseparably interwoven in this story. But we naturally turn to that of the main protagonist in this book, Sir Arthur Conan Doyle—doctor, novelist, playwright, creator of ' Brigadier Gerard ' and ' Sherlock Holmes,' military historian, patriot, traveller, sportsman, supporter of humane causes, finally leader of the Spiritualist movement and lecturer throughout the English-speaking world. His varied life, his immense activity, and extraordinary personality have been the subject of three biographies since his passing in 1930; even so, it may be that in these days the public have almost forgotten his variety and accomplishment—save only the fact that he created the modern vogue for the detective story !

As a boy the present writer looked forward each month to the arrival of a monthly magazine bearing on its cover a picture of the Strand, London, with a hansom cab in the foreground, and a long vista of other horse-drawn vehicles. At the end of the *Strand Magazine* were entrancing fairy stories by E. Nesbit, sometimes about a creature such as was never seen on land or sea called a ' Psammead.' Also there appeared stories by one, Arthur Conan Doyle, concerning the adventures of Sherlock Holmes, ostensibly related by a Doctor Watson. Little did he realise that here before his very eyes were all but the first and certainly the very best of all detective stories, not to be equalled, far less surpassed by others in the subsequent spate of detective stories which they originated. Nor did the actual name Arthur Conan Doyle mean much to him until in later years he read his *Stark Munro Letters*, a book which is more or less autobiographical. Its author seemed so British in his uncompromising love of truth, sincerity, and enthusiasm for sport and action and love of country. Also he had the knack of catching and holding his reader's interest with the first sentence of a story, of bringing a character to life in a sentence or two. Not until years afterwards did it become plain that this vividness occurred because the writer was himself living in his characters, that he was born to his trade, and that his books were veritable expressions of himself. Also they were eminently readable because of their technical skill. Conan Doyle himself once said that his writing was at its best but plain English. But how plain an English was this, how forceful and sincere a style! It is not surprising that stories such as ' Silver Blaze ' and the ' Brigadier Gerard ' series came to be hailed as literary masterpieces of their time.

Arthur Conan Doyle was born in Edinburgh on the 22nd of May, 1859. He died on the 7th of July, 1930. During his 71 years of vigorous life he wrote about forty full-length books, several plays, a history of the South African War, and another of the First World War in six volumes (two major works, the writing of which might occupy a lesser writer for years), together with almost innumerable short stories of a quality which never flagged. His athletic achievements were no less notable.

He excelled at boxing, played cricket for the M.C.C. at Lords, was a pioneer motorist, an expert at billiards, and the introducer of Norwegian skiing into Switzerland. It seems that whereas the ordinary man lives only a life half-alive, this man lived throughout his days with a full hundred-per-cent vigour and enthusiasm. Even during his last illness Sir Arthur occupied himself by drawing a pencil sketch which he called ' The Old Horse '—depicting himself as the old horse drawing the formidable load of his lifetime's achievement along a road where outstanding incidents of his career took the place of milestones. These included his school and university days, his adventures in a whaler, his medical practice, his mountaineering adventures, lecturing tours in America, activities during the Boer War, electioneering, and world tours as a propagandist for Spiritualism. Piled to a colossal height on the wagon were hosts of his books, short stories, plays, and so on, together with a series of 500 lectures, the whole topped up by an array of golf clubs, boxing gloves, a cricket bat, billiard cues, skis, and other instruments symbolic of his love of sport.

The picture was an epitome of his life, about which, as we have said, no less than three biographies have appeared since his death. Yet the burden the old horse draws largely omits the activity into which he poured his utmost energy, health, and finances, and which finally curtailed his life. This mission led him to deny almost everything that he had attained—wealth, ease, comfort, home-life, recognition and fame, even a peerage which was offered him—for the sake of an unpopular conviction which demanded all that he had left to give to life. We learn from his books that he had been interested in psychical research for many years. He had investigated several haunted houses and some poltergeist cases, and had met with startling experiences. ' Starting,' he says, ' from a position of comparative materialism I had at least become receptive and continued to investigate in the leisure hours of a very busy life.*

' But when the (first World) War came it brought earnestness into all our souls and made us look more closely at our own

---

* This quotation is from his book, *The New Revelation*.

beliefs and reassess their values. In the presence of an agonised world, hearing every day of the deaths of the flower of our race in the first promise of their unfulfilled youth, seeing around one the wives and mothers who had no clear conception whither their loved one had gone, I suddenly seemed to see that this subject with which I had so long dallied was not merely the study of a force outside the rules of science but that it was really something tremendous, a breaking down of the walls between two worlds, a direct undeniable message from beyond, a call of hope and guidance for the human race at the time of its deepest affliction.'

In this passage were expressed the writer's fearless confession of faith, and his conviction that here was the most important of all subjects open for man to study. Later came the additional conviction that here was something in the nature of a basic revelation. If death ended all for every person, then a person had lived for no purpose, since all his ideals, his hopes, achievements, affections, longings and the deep call of his heart for God all ended in extinction. So it must be with the host who had sacrificed their lives in Flanders. For if the individual man lived in vain then Christ also had lived and died in vain, for man had no soul to save. So also with the other world teachers; equally vain were the various faiths or religions they had inspired. St. Paul's cry, ' O grave, where is thy victory? O death, where is thy sting?' was meaningless. Without survival all that remains for man is to practise some system of morality (such as that of Confucius); and systems of morality are cold comfort for the loss of a million men during a war—a war which in itself constituted the breakdown of international morality.

These were the realisations that spurred Arthur Conan Doyle onward. He was then the highest paid of short story writers—at the rate of ten shillings a word; but now his income must go, except for an occasional short story; no more books must be written save on psychic matters, with survival as their theme. Boldly, trenchantly, he affirmed his new faith. 'Conan Doyle!'— went up the public cry of amazement—' He, of all men, to believe in this sort of thing!'

It mattered little what people said. Everything had to go.

This was his calling, his crusade. Then began those tours (accompanied by his family) when the glad tidings had to be told across the world. For eleven years he drove himself on exhausting lecture tours through Australia, South Africa, America and Britain, never sparing himself, and latterly heedless of warnings by his doctors. No man in his sixties could stand the strain. One of the last acts of his life was to struggle up to London to head a deputation to the Home Secretary about the centuries-old-law under which spiritualist mediums were prosecuted. Then came the end. Within a few days, the warrior was spent; his sword of the spirit was laid down at last.

His remains were laid in the garden of his home near Crowborough, near the hut where most of his stories were written.† It is said that the gathering was more like a quiet garden party than a funeral, for summer dresses were worn, and few people were in mourning. A huge crowd attended, and a host of telegrams poured in. A special train brought flowers. It seemed that his friends were world-wide.

Thus was his body laid to rest. The flowers that had been sent covered the whole field. On the headstone was later inscribed his name, the date of his birth and four words:

' Steel true, blade straight.'

Mr. John Dickson Carr's book, *The Life of Sir Arthur Conan Doyle*★, ends with these words, 'Let no man write his epitaph. He is not dead.'

It is true. Both his name and reputation have survived. In almost every bookshop will be found ' omnibus ' volumes of his short stories, mostly the *Sherlock Holmes* series, and his books are frequently serialised over the air. Only books such as *The White Company* and *Sir Nigel*, and those about Spiritualism have fallen into the background, and these were dearest of all to their writer. Those books of his which have entertainment value look like continuing for years to come; his deeper and more thoughtful books—not these.

' He is not dead.' He lives on in these pages. Here is his final message.

★Published by John Murray. †Since moved to Minstead Church, Hampshire.

CHAPTER III

MINESTA

'Keep that light in your eye and go up directly thereto; so shalt thou see the gate.'
—John Bunyan.

'The sharp edge of a razor, hard to traverse; a difficult path is this —thus the wise say.'
—Katha Upanishad.

THE late eighteen hundreds were the days of large families. To one of these a little girl was born, who came as the ninth child with a gap of five years between herself and the child before her. Her mother died when she was only seven years of age, and the intrusion of death in so poignant a form at so tender an age left memories, which she has never wholly forgotten, of her own loss through death. Having felt the sting of bereavement so early, her sympathy with others in similar circumstances has always been keen, and her desire to help and comfort them strengthened.

It appears that during her long illness the mother discussed with her husband the possibility of human survival after death, and the wife promised to communicate with him, if this were possible, after her passing. This for two staunch Nonconformists living in Victorian days shows a certain enlightenment.

Some time after his wife had passed on, the husband was taken by a friend to the home of a noted medium, Mrs. Annie Boddington. The two men sat at the back of the room, listening to the address, after which the medium gave 'clairvoyance,' or 'spirit messages,' to various persons in her audience. None came to the bereaved husband; but as he was unobtrusively leaving, the medium asked if the gentleman then going out would wait. He did so, and afterwards she came to him saying she had seen clairvoyantly that he had recently lost his wife, and that her spirit, waiting in the room to speak to him, had stood aside until the other people had gone—a form of timidity characteristic of her. Then the medium began to speak, as from the wife, giving the husband a message to each of her children by name, and showing by further evidence that she was conversant with all that had been happening in the home since her passing. What was so strangely convincing, however, was that while she was giving these messages the medium's hands were carefully arranging and rearranging the handkerchief in the husband's outside breast pocket; for this had always been a habit of the wife's.

Can it be wondered that the husband returned home walking on air, with never a doubt that his wife had fulfilled her promise, and that he had spoken to her? His certainty was shared by all his children, then mostly in their late teens. Forthwith the whole family became Spiritualists, and the father an ardent advocate and worker in the movement. In course of time he was speaking at one or other of the Spiritualist churches or halls every week. Those were the days when to affirm oneself a Spiritualist required courage. A Spiritualist might be abused in the street, or even have missiles flung at him; while church services were frequently interrupted by stones coming through the windows or by bricks thrown onto the roof. Spiritualist mediums, moreover, were continually being prosecuted under an Act for the 'suppression of witches' dating back to the middle ages.

Of course, the little girl, Grace, also became a Spiritualist. At an early age she attended the movement's Lyceum or Sunday School, since when she has never wavered in her certainty of survival and reunion.

This certainty, however, has not been based on messages received through other mediums, although she is familiar with this procedure, regarding it as natural and normal. Some are born to music, drama, painting or song, with gifts or faculties which are inherent and must be given expression if they are not to languish or die. Grace had perhaps the rarest faculty of all; for she was a natural born psychic, with gifts of clairvoyance, of second sight or prediction, of spiritual sensitiveness, and of power to diagnose and heal sickness, which needed no developing, for they were spontaneous. These gifts were encouraged, of course, by her family's and her own familiarity with Spiritualism. They might easily have been crushed had she been born into some harder-headed materialistic family. But their use to her was as natural as breathing, and they manifested spontaneously. She was no more than thirteen when she gave a description and message to a woman (whom she had met for the first time) from someone who had died. She remembers telling the amazed woman that she was about to cross the seas to a distant land, where she would live in a house surrounded by a broad verandah on three sides. Afterwards little Grace was told that she had described some dearly loved relative of the woman who had died, and given her a message she would never forget, especially as she was just about to return to her home in South Africa. One can imagine how impressive this communication must have been coming through a child who was a stranger.

After her mother's death Grace's life was none of the easiest. Her brothers and sisters were out in the world by now; her father had married again, not very happily. She was left alone for long hours in a big house in a somewhat lonely part of South London; and being an intensely sensitive child she was often frightened. But at such times a visitor whom she called the ' old man ' would occasionally come and talk to her and comfort her. She remembers that he did not look like an ordinary person but rather as if he carried some sort of light inside him: it shone out so that he seemed illumined. After he had been with her she would fall asleep and dream happily; and so natural did the visitant seem to the child that it was not until later that she realised that he was not actually of this world.

Thus, though she lacked human society and made few friends of her own age, another order of existence offered her companionship. She grew to love that other world and her desire to serve its interests became a dominant factor in her life. So it was that in her late teens she appeared on the Spiritualist platform to give an address and clairvoyance; and as the simplicity and youth of the exponent created something of a sensation she was asked, in the years that followed, to speak at other centres. Eventually a week rarely passed without several of these engagements.

This was hard work, for it involved journeys about and across London, and also to provincial towns or cities such as Birmingham, Edinburgh or Glasgow. In fact, most of such engagements meant a wearisome Sunday journey, the giving of an address and clairvoyance, an even more wearisome return home, with little more in the way of material recompense than enough to cover expenses. This called for devotion to a self-imposed duty over a number of years. It was worth while, for the effort developed qualities of courage and steadfastness which were to fit her for the work that lay in the future, and brought her even nearer in spirit to her teacher and guide.

Every medium, it is said, has a guide, or ' doorkeeper,' in the unseen world who acts as guardian, counsellor and friend. These are often coloured folk; and this may seem strange to the westerner who is convinced that some white-skinned person would do just as well or better. But the westerner is apt to concentrate on intellectual development rather than intelligence; and there is a difference between these: indeed it is often the case that the more highly developed a man's intellect, the less intelligent he is. It would seem that intelligence is the quality needed in a guide; meaning that gentle wisdom which comes by living close to God. It is often discarnate people of the red and yellow races, the Tibetans, Indians, Chinese, Red Indians, who manifest this wisdom of the heart.

It has been suggested that the visitor who used to comfort the child Grace when she was alone and frightened was not of this world. He was, in fact, the child's guide or mentor, given this charge from her birth. His name, she learnt later, was White Eagle.

During all the many years the writer has known White Eagle, he has been extraordinarily reticent about himself, his past and his present mission. He says that he is just a friend to all, an old man who drops in because he likes to help people in their troubles. Maybe he is wiser than some of us because he stands a little higher and can see a little further, and thus knows what is going to happen.

White Eagle's contact with his medium is always by a process of projection. He lives, we have learned, in the mountains of the East, and he can project either himself or his influence half across the world to her, by functioning, like other initiates, in the ethereal body. So while he lives in a physical body, as do other initiates, he is able (as are they) to function in the ethereal world which pervades this physical globe, of which the latter is the replica. In that ethereal world (the real *living* world, in which our world of the senses is cradled) there is neither time nor space as we know it. Therefore he need not journey half across the sense-world to get anywhere. At once he can be at any one place, or contact any one person, or answer someone's call for help. Only with the resumption of the physical or sense body does the Sage resume or take on himself our mortal limitations and our burden. Not even then to the same degree as man. The Sage's body is perfected, is no longer subjected to weariness, sickness or death as we know these things.

It is a habit of White Eagle's to bestow a new name on his friends, and one which usually seems to fit them better than the name with which they were christened. Sometimes it is the name of a Biblical character, such as Peter, Matthew or Luke, or a name from The Pilgrim's Progress. Sometimes it will denote some dominant trait in the personality or stimulate some quality which the personality needs. These ' soul ' or ' character ' names carry with them, moreover, an inkling of what is to be expected from the person concerned. A Peter, a Luke, or a John will display qualities, shortcomings or virtues, similar to those of their prototypes in the Gospels. Indeed it often happens that the new name will presently supersede the old one, and a man becomes known by it among his friends.

The name which White Eagle bestowed on his medium is ' Minesta,' which means ' mother '; we shall see later how apt this name has been. From now on it will be convenient to refer to the medium, otherwise Mrs. Grace Cooke, by the name of Minesta.

Minesta had been conducting services and giving clairvoyance each Sunday, and often on weekdays for about twenty years on behalf of Spiritualism. During these years her powers of clair-voyance and vision must have carried conviction to some thousands of people. Thus, the influence of her work had gone far and wide.

To contact and to serve the higher intelligence a medium must be a person of unusual and purposefully cultivated sensibility, and with qualities of character—of mind, motive and feeling—without which his or her gifts could never function. This is why so long a period of hard work and endurance was necessary to toughen and at the same time refine her character even while at the same time her sensitivity was increasing by reason of her work.

At the end of these years of what may be called preparation Minesta had reached middle life, and was married with two children and a home to look after. By then, however, the nature of her work had changed somewhat in consequence of a meeting with Miss Estelle Stead, daughter of the famous journalist, W. T. Stead (who went down in the *Titanic*), and leader of the ' Stead Borderland Library,' regarded as one of the important centres of the Spiritualist movement in London, and where Minesta went several times a week. Her task now was mainly to help and convince recently bereaved people of survival. Many of these were torn by grief and sometimes so embittered that it required a great effort to raise them out of despair.

The Stead Library was situated in Smith Square, Westminster; and a few hundred yards away in Victoria Street, facing the Abbey, was Sir Arthur Conan Doyle's ' Psychic Bookshop,' which he had opened some years before—aiming not only to supply the general public but animated by the hope that clergy from the Abbey might drop in to purchase psychic books. It is doubtful if any ever did. The Bookshop, which was in the charge of his daughter Mary, must have involved Sir Arthur in a very considerable loss for several years. It was not long before such near-neighbours as the Stead Library and the Book-shop—and also Minesta and Miss Mary Conan Doyle—became acquainted. A friendship soon sprang up between the two, resulting in an invitation to Minesta from Sir Arthur and Lady

Doyle to visit them at their home near Crowborough in Sussex. Sir Arthur, on hearing about Minesta's work for Spiritualism, and about White Eagle (and especially the latter) was deeply anxious to meet Minesta.

This happened during the summer of 1930 when Sir Arthur was a very sick man. A week-end visit was arranged, and then suddenly cancelled because a turn for the worse came. Soon followed the news of Sir Arthur's passing—a great shock—for he seemed a very part of the Britain of those days.

Every one of these seemingly trivial details about Minesta and Sir Arthur have their significance, for they denote a linking, a drawing together of the two even before his passing. They never met; but they had a community of interests, a likeness of purpose at that time. To the world and to themselves they were as strangers; and yet their lives were interwoven even then by ties destined to draw them closer in the near future.

CHAPTER IV

THE HERMIT OF BAGNAIA

' If you call me by day or night by these names I will come to
assist and to help; the Angel will come to assist and help; and the
Spirits also come.'

—The Avesta.

' May they who have attained the spiritual life, gentle and righteous,
aid us when we call them.'

—Rig Veda.

THE third tributary story which merges into the main current of
events is that of the Hermit of Bagnaia—a small town near
Viterbo, about sixty miles north of Rome. This account is
translated from the *Bulletin des Polaires* for June 9th, 1930.*

' Following many enquiries as to the circumstances which
surrounded the transmission of the Oracle de Force Astrale by
Father Julian to his successor, we have much pleasure in citing
briefly where and how this moving episode took place:

' In 1908 a young man found himself during his vacation at
Bagnaia, a pleasant country town of Viterbais in the neighbourhood of Rome.

' No sooner had he arrived than his attention was drawn to
an old man wearing the coarse monkish habit. Tall, ascetic,
sunburnt, his eyes deep set, he passed along the streets as though
in a dream.

' The lad made enquiries from the country folk. Was this man
a godly hermit? No. After listening to what was said, he
gathered that this individual, who was called Father Julian, was

---

* LE BULLETIN DES POLAIRES was published from May 9th, 1930 onwards
by the ' Groupe des Polaires ' during their existence in Paris (their headquarters
being for several years at 36 Avenue Junot, 18e). For additional details see
the book published earlier: ASIA MYSTERIOSA. *L'Oracle de Force Astrale comme
moyen de communication avec les " Petites Lumières d'Orient."* Par Zam Bhotiva.
1929. (Dorban-Ainé, Editeur, 19 Boulevard Haussmann, Paris, 9e).

considered by the dwellers in this little town as one who could cast magical spells—a sorcerer. Although nothing definite in the way of accusation could be brought against him the " presumptions " seemed grave—it would be as well, they said, to beware of this strange person, who lived as a wild man of the woods in an old ruined hut and fed on herbs and fruits; who was scorned by all good Christians and was, moreover, one who had never been seen to cross the threshold of the House of God. Things had come to such a pitch that finally it had been pointed out to him, and not too politely, that it might be as well if he did not loiter in passing by the vines or corn fields, for very potent spells, capable of drying up the ripe grapes or of destroying the cattle by a mysterious disease, can be quickly cast.

' In spite of these tales of magical charms and evil spells the young man was greatly drawn to the recluse, by a strange sympathy, and one day he decided to visit him in his hut. He was received as one who had been expected for a long time. The lad offered money—clothing—a more suitable shelter. The hermit refused in his curiously deep and slightly guttural voice, a voice, nevertheless, full of great sweetness; he intimated that he found all he required in the woods around him; the herbs and fruits necessary to him as food; the running streams to drink from. Besides, he *must* stay where he was even in spite of the hostility of those around him, until the day came for him to set out on a long, a very long, journey.

' The next day the young man paid another visit with eagerness; and never a day passed without a meeting—during which the hermit would speak of Goodness, of True Love, and of Brotherhood. Truly, this young Roman boy, firmly attached though he was to the things of the world, saw in the recluse an initiate and partly understood the gentle foolishness of his self-imposed isolation—his way of life—hard and painful though it appeared outwardly, as well as his firm resolve to refuse all outside aid.

' The boy was moved by such sympathy and profound pity for the recluse, so good and of such sweetness of nature, that he felt it an almost sacred duty to continue his daily pilgrimage to him.

' One day on going up the path to the hermit's dwelling, he found Father Julian lying unconscious on the road, badly wounded in the knee. He dressed the deep wound as well as he was able, and then assisted the old man to re-enter his hut. The next day he found the hermit up and about; three days later the wound was completely healed.

' What mysterious herbs had been the means of obtaining this complete restoration to health? The young man did not dare to inquire. Many a time the recluse when questioned somewhat indiscreetly by his young friend would remain silent, lost in a dream, the reflection of which shone through his large, dark, far-seeing eyes.

' The link which united the two men grew stronger and stronger. The visits to the hermit's cell became more frequent, the conversations between them of greater length and of a more intimate nature. The old man spoke meaningly of pain and sacrifice to the younger man whose eyes were still fixed on the dreams and illusions of life. At length the end of the holidays was at hand. With a saddened heart the youth made his way for the last time to the hermit's abode. It will never be known what the recluse murmured "from mouth to ear" to him whom he called for the first time "his son." We can only say that at the moment of leave-taking, he handed to him some leaves of paper yellowed by the passage of time. These were " a small fragment from the Book of the Science of Life and of Death."

' The recipient of these mysterious pages will remember to the end of his days the last words spoken to him by the Sage: " Should you at any time require help or counsel you have only to follow the instructions which are contained in this old manuscript—*you will receive your reply*. It may even occur that one day *I myself will reply to you*. But remember never to divulge to anyone in the world what is written on these pages, for in so doing you run the risk for yourself, as well as for the one who obtains the knowledge, of madness or death."

' The pages contained an arithmetical system which permitted an answer to whatever question was formulated. The youth who had little or no inclination to dive into occult mysteries, put away the manuscript in a place of safety, without even having had sufficient curiosity to consult the marvellous Oracle.

'It was not until two years later that the young man, who was then in great distress of mind, made use of the strange power which had been confided to him by Father Julian. He consulted the manuscript. It was necessary first to dwell very strongly upon one's wish, to write it down and to supply the surname and Christian name of the one making the enquiry and also the names of his mother. He formulated his question and then spent long hours in the prescribed arithmetical calculations.

'The reply obtained showed itself to be astonishingly correct and to contain great wisdom.

'Amazed at this result the custodian of the Oracle some time later spoke to a group of his friends, who were students of the esoteric, of this strange method of obtaining information. Thus the groups came into being. In 1923 Father Julian kept his promise. He replied himself.

'In April, 1930, by means of the Oracle de Force Astrale he sent his last message in the flesh ' to his well-beloved sons.'

'And now the Lord Buddha has opened to him the Path of Light.'

Here the account of how the Oracle de Force Astrale came to be used comes to an end. A complete outline of how it worked cannot now be given. This no one knows. The system was communicated, fulfilled its appointed purpose, and has now ceased. It could only be operated apparently by someone possessing the requisite psychic or soul-vibration, which perhaps one in ten thousand might have, the youth being one of these; doubtless for this reason he was brought to Father Julian. This is why what follows must seem somewhat sketchy and inadequate. What is quite certain is that the oracle worked and that its message had a cogency and power which made it unique.

It was operated, as has been said, by arithmetical calculation. So does the ancient science of Astrology operate, although the intuition of the astrologer plays its part. No doubt the intuition of the operator of the Force Astrale was equally important when he was sending or receiving messages.

God, it is said, geometrises, for He is the great Geometrician of the Universe. In other words, the universe of God's creation could be reduced to a geometrical or mathematical formula were there any mathematicians capable enough! In a like manner man's own inventions have to be reduced to formulae before they can be constructed. Much the same principle lay behind the Force Astrale.

For instance, any person asking a question through it had to think out the question very clearly and write it down in the fewest possible words. He had also to supply his full name and date of birth, together with his mother's maiden name and her date of birth. The question had then to be translated into Italian, because the Force Astrale operated only in that language. The first task of the operator (now a grown man, and known to his intimates as the 'Mage' or magician) was to turn each *letter* of the words of the question, together with the *names* of the questioner and his mother, into arithmetical figures. He then, by intricate calculations and by use of his own psychic power, 'sent out' this question and obtained an answer to it, the latter coming in as a mass of figures meaning nothing to the Mage until translated back into letters and so into words. From a short question a long answer might come, and vice versa. Sometimes even a long course of instruction or advice would come through. It was claimed that the mind of the operator in no way influenced or affected the quality of the message as might the subconscious mind of a medium. That is as may be. What is certain is that the instructions were accepted without question.

It can be imagined how dumbfounded was the young man at this discovery and how eager he and a friend were to communicate again with Father Julian. What they wanted to know now was the why and wherefore of the secret and why it had been entrusted to them in particular. Many hours were spent in communication, which, it is plain, must by reason of the procedure entailed, have necessarily been slow and laborious.

A later message through the Force Astrale bade the two men go to Paris and there establish a group which should be called the Polaire Brotherhood. They arrived—strangers in a strange city—and almost penniless. Mysteriously, people introduced themselves and became friends. Money was supplied, and soon the Brotherhood occupied handsome premises in the Avenue Junot on the western slopes of Montmartre. The *Bulletin des Polaires*, a monthly magazine, ultimately reached a circulation of ten thousand copies among adherents of the Polaire Brotherhood.

All this was happening, it should be noted, some few years after the first ' War which was to end War.' At that time the nations were too busy putting their world together again to bother themselves much over the possibility of war in the future. Armed forces were everywhere being disbanded. It is therefore disconcerting to find that the early messages communicated through the Force Astrale referred to the ' Years of Fire ' that were surely coming on the world (if it did not change its ways), and which would involve an era of destruction and privation far exceeding that just experienced. But after these particular communications no more came from Father Julian, who, having as it were established relations, disappeared. Thereafter the communicator was someone carrying greater weight and authority, who became known as the Chevalier Rose-Croix, the Chevalier Sage or the Wise Knight (he has been later identified as the Master ' R ' who, as it is well known, was once the Brother Francis Bacon). The Force Astrale had been entrusted to the young man by way of preparation against the coming of the Years of Fire. Henceforward the Wise Knight was to be leader; the Force Astrale his means of communication.

A word about the Masters. Long ago, an occult tradition tells us, the area of land and sea around the North Pole was not only habitable but possessed of a warm and genial climate. It was referred to by the Greeks as the Hyperborean region, where there had once dwelt advanced men (and, of course, women) known as Masters; that is, having become masters over them-selves—over their human weaknesses—they were no longer subject to the limitations of time or space as men know them. They were masters of time, and over age, illness and death. While they could live as man lives on the physical plane, they could also lay aside their physical bodies (leaving them in a profound slumber or trance, as do some of the Indian mystics today), and function in unseen worlds such as the after-death states. Long, long ago when the earth was young and innocent they ruled it by loving-kindness. Theirs was the golden age to which folk tales such as the Garden of Eden story refer. But then some interstellar convulsion shifted the earth on its axis, and a tide of ice and snow followed, which slowly enveloped the polar regions; and co-incident with this, the golden age chilled and hardened into one of materialism, before whose advance the Sages retreated to the mountains of the far East, where in secluded fastnesses they are established to this day, no longer mingling with the world of men, unable to endure man's present vibrations.

Tidings of these Masters occasionally reach the peoples of the East, most of whom have heard about and believe in them. Some years ago the writer met a professor from one of the Indian Universities visiting Britain, and in conversation heard him tell of his meeting with a Master. When asked what he was like, the professor simply answered, 'He is all love.'

In these words we have the keynote of a Master or Initiate. Since they no longer mingle with men, their love is now expressed by a projection of light, which is a ray of love; for love takes the form of light when sent out to mankind—and also to certain chosen and responsible individuals, who may or may not be aware of their contact with a Master. By this power of projection which they possess they are able to inspire, to strengthen, to raise such people (if they be willing) but never to influence unduly or override the free will choice and volition of any human soul. The symbol of the Polar Star given to the Polaires was therefore an ancient symbol descended from Hyperborean times, countless centuries ago, and still possessing some of its ancient power. The Oracle de Force Astrale may date back as long. So also might the method and organisation of the Polaire Brotherhood itself be modelled on one far in the past. In any case instructions were given how to make use of the methods of projection employed by the Masters—but with a difference; for the Brotherhood groups must perforce work on a human ray or wave-length instead of that of the Initiates. Thus, when at its meetings the Brotherhood received the ray of the Masters it was able to 'tune down' the latter and project it forth again on another wave-length likely to be efficacious with more worldly men and women. We have to recognise that any group of some sixty people such as this, who were animated by one purpose, who had been trained over the years, who were unified and harmonised by methods which enhanced that purpose and fortified by greater powers behind, could not be without influence in the land.

We have to bear in mind that well before the late nineteen-twenties the Sages never doubted the coming of a second world war. They knew also something of its extent and horrors. Their plans to help must have been made at least as long ago as the boy's meeting with Father Julian, which resulted in knowledge of the Force Astrale being given to the boy.

Before the reason for the formation of a Polaire Brotherhood can be realised we have to recognise the real nature of war. Most people think it is primarily waged with armies, navies, or in the air; with bombs, guns and every devilish device man can exploit. But any armed conflict is but an *effect* resulting from some underlying causes which must first possess men's minds and hearts and rule their emotions. When over a term of years men's minds are inflamed, their fears fomented, their distrust and presently hatred of other nations aggravated, the whole one day reaches boiling point and expresses itself in conflict between armies. This is but a plain sequence of cause and effect.

War really originates, it is here suggested, in men's minds and souls years before its actual outbreak. This thesis seems almost unanswerable; it also reveals the reason not only why the Masters were sure that war was coming— since they have power to read the mass-mind or soul of the nations; but also why they formed a Brotherhood trained to work on that mass-mind.

They did not promise at any time that the war would be averted. The karma of the world by then had almost ensured its coming. They said only that the margin between victory and defeat for the forces of the light might be so narrow that the work of the Brotherhood could turn the scale.

The Polaires were, as has been said, engaged in ' good works,' which differed widely from the ' good works ' of orthodoxy. They did not pray aloud as at a prayer meeting. They did not make great *mental* efforts to project the light; theirs was rather a relaxing, an opening of themselves to receive the Master's ray so that it might flow through them. To whom or what was the ray re-directed? To help someone in trouble occasionally, but mostly to groups or communities or nations threatened or smitten by misfortune or catastrophe in any part of the world. Or the Brotherhood projection might be directed to individuals or to groups of people working for peace, for freedom, or for any other good cause. They worked also for lost souls after death. The tasks which engaged the Brotherhood were of this nature; while in their daily round or common task the individual Brothers tried to fulfil their obligation to be helpful to their fellows.

Part of the Polaire ' charge ' or ' obligation ' was that the Polaires must strive to remove the *mad fear of death which haunts the brain of man*—mark, the *brain* of man; perhaps his heart knows better? This brings us to the year 1930 when news of Sir Arthur Conan Doyle's death reached France. Towards the end of 1930 a long message was received through the Force Astrale from the Wise Knight relating to it. Sir Arthur, the message said, had communicated with the Sages, seeking their aid. Since his arrival in the spirit land he had found that much of what he had previously thought true about Spiritualism (of which movement he had been the leader) and of the conditions of the next life needed revision. He desired to correct any errors which he had sponsored. At the moment he was not in a position to do this, as certain ties still held his soul to earth. His passionate desire was to make these corrections. This he could not do alone. Such was the importance of his message that everything must be done to ensure its accurate reception. This could not be done through the Force Astrale. A certain member of the Brotherhood was therefore directed to proceed to England and to get into touch with Lady Conan Doyle, who would then introduce him to the medium through whom the Wise Knight desired the message to come. This medium, it was stated, had been long chosen and trained for this particular task. When he met her the Polaire Brother would recognise her at once. Let there be no delay.

CHAPTER V

THE MESSENGER FROM FRANCE

' To give religion a foundation of rock instead of quicksand, to remove the legitimate doubts of earnest minds, to make the invisible forces with their moral reactions a real thing, and to re-assure the human race as to the future which awaits it—surely no more glorious message was ever heralded to mankind.'

—Arthur Conan Doyle, *The Wanderings of a Spiritualist.*

THESE lines are written on January 27th, 1956. Twenty-five years ago, again on January 27th, a group consisting of Lady Conan Doyle, her family, and three friends, a Monsieur Zam Bhotiva from Paris, Minesta and her husband, met at the Stead Library in Smith Square, Westminster. Whether there is any significance in the fact that this account is being written on the same date in January depends on how far *numbers* influence human lives. For some people become aware that their lives react to numbers in a strange way. For instance, things mostly seem to happen to them on certain days of the week or month. We receive a number at birth—our date and year, and we vibrate to it; each of us being a unit in the mathematical, or geometrical, scheme of the universe. The Force Astrale, for example, was intimately concerned with numbers and depended on arithmetical calculations for its efficacy. Indeed, it operated on a three-six-nine vibration (nine being thought to be the number of the initiate.) The six-pointed star given to the Polaires as their symbol was of course a *six*-vibration. This is why the Brotherhood, aware that it must conform to the three-six-nine vibration for its best work, usually chose a three-six-nine day of the month and hour of the day for its principal activities, and at first adopted a diagram depicting the figures ' three-six-nine ' as an emblem for the heading of the *Bulletin des Polaires.*

28

Minesta also was born on the ninth day of the sixth month, and was also a ninth child. Here also we have the three-six-nine vibration evident in her life. Sir Arthur Conan Doyle was born on the 22nd May: May is the fifth month of the year; the two two's of the 22nd added together make four, and the four coupled with five make nine, so here the three-six-nine vibration becomes evident again. It is perhaps worth mentioning that the compiler and editor of this book was also born on May 22nd, because this 365-to-1 chance might have significance. Finally, we note that all the Conan Doyle work and messages began on the twenty-seventh day of the month, which is a day of three-times-three, making nine, and three times nine making 27.

The first message from Sir Arthur—whom we will call ' A.C.D.' henceforth for the sake of brevity—came on January 27th, 1931, and initiated a long series of messages in which he set forth a full restatement of Spiritualism; making it clear once and for all that death and survival (and occasional communication between the worlds) can be regarded as a normal and natural experience, as much part of human life as the love between man and woman or the birth of a child. Those who read his message intelligently and receptively should lose the fear of death.

Within a few days of A.C.D.'s passing, the Spiritualists held a Memorial Service at the Albert Hall to commemorate their leader. Many hundreds were turned away. It would be interesting to know how many of the thousands gathered there to demonstrate their very genuine grief and their reverence for his service to their cause had been convinced of survival by his own mighty effort for Spiritualism over the years. They might well have numbered half of those present, so powerful had been A.C.D.'s advocacy for Spiritualism. About this time many of the leaders of Spiritualism met to discuss proposals designed to commemorate A.C.D.'s work for the movement. A million-shilling fund was one of these, and nobody saw a limit to what might be accomplished. We shall return to what actually *was* accomplished later.

Ten days after A.C.D.'s passing Minesta paid her first visit to his home in Crowborough, where she was welcomed by

Lady Conan Doyle and the family. Shortly after a death the soul of the person concerned can be readily seen by a 'sensitive' or 'psychic.' This was the case with A.C.D. who joined his family in their welcome to Minesta, but was seen by her alone. Incidentally, it must be hard when a man who has passed over seeks desperately to make contact with his relatives, and they shut him out because of prejudice or fear, religious or otherwise. A.C.D. spoke to all of them that night through Minesta, not yet himself controlling the medium, but with White Eagle acting as his spokesman. The message was both intimate and detailed. A family reunion took place so strong that none present could doubt or question it.

A stranger in these matters may want to know how a 'dead' man can speak to his family. The process is natural enough; but it can only become possible through a close co-operation between medium and guide, which comes only after long training and constant practice. It should be explained that communication between White Eagle and his medium takes two forms: either he may draw very close and bring her under a powerful ray of thought or inspiration, when she will speak the message he desires to send through; or he may bring her under his control, so that she falls into a state resembling the natural sleep of a child. This is by far the stronger, however, being a trance-state so deep that she has no knowledge of what is said while it lasts and no recollection afterwards. It is then that White Eagle himself speaks through her. Her voice changes, deepening in tone; and she speaks with a slight accent, a changed delivery and choice of words. Moreover, the mind and personality of the speaker is strongly marked and there is even a facial change, so complete is the fade-out of the personality of Minesta. No one could doubt that it is now one of the opposite sex who speaks.

The awakening out of this trance-state is as natural as the awakening from sleep. Minesta normally remembers nothing of what has happened. If she shortly afterwards reads a record of what was said through her lips a faint memory stirs, much like the recollection of a dream during waking hours; and that is all.

On some occasions White Eagle stands aside for someone other than himself to speak through his medium; but more usually he passes the messages on himself. White Eagle thus played a major part in the transmission of the earlier messages from A.C.D. to his family; but this is no less convincing because not only the personal message but some of his mannerisms, habitual terms of expression and so forth would come through from the communicator. This was the more cogent proof, since Minesta had not met A.C.D. during his lifetime.*

As a result a prolonged correspondence followed at irregular intervals between Minesta and Lady Conan Doyle. Sir Arthur evidently meant to keep an eye on the happenings at his home, for many a word of advice or caution came through with his messages of affection to the family. Lady Doyle's letters show how well these were understood and appreciated.

Nevertheless, even at this early stage there was an element of dissatisfaction in Minesta's mind. The messages themselves, she felt, despite their detailed precision, had not the drive and force which might be expected of someone like A.C.D. Probably this passed unnoticed by everyone but Minesta herself. Meanwhile, a representative committee of Spiritualists was meeting to discuss the Memorial, and after weeks of debate, during which public enthusiasm cooled, more or less reached a deadlock. About this time, Minesta spent a few days at the Doyle family ' cottage ' at Bignall Wood in the New Forest; and during her visit A.C.D. spoke with some vigour about the Memorial, saying it was necessary to get down to business. He then named those whom he wished to serve on the Memorial Committee, the most notable, so far as this book is concerned, being Mr. W. R. Bradbrook of Ipswich, who became honorary secretary. Despite the latter's enthusiasm and drive many difficulties held up progress. The appeal was not launched until the Armistice Day of 1930, when a copy lay on every seat at the Spiritualist Service of

---

* It has not been thought necessary in the present work to give all the circumstantial details or even the whole text of the early messages which were fully reported in the book, *Thy Kingdom Come*, by Ivan Cooke. (Published by Wright & Brown, London.)

Remembrance at the Albert Hall—where A.C.D. had dragged himself a year before to deliver what was almost his last message to the public.

What was the result? Appeals were inserted in twenty-six psychic journals in many countries. Forty thousand copies of the appeal were distributed in magazines to which A.C.D. had been a frequent contributor. Some hundreds of letters were posted to 'key' persons, asking for support, and the several hundred Spiritualist churches in Britain were approached. Sixteen months later the net result stood at about two thousand pounds, a sum which included an anonymous gift of several hundred pounds. This meant that funds were insufficient to attempt to carry out the aims set forth in the appeal, and to all intents and purposes it had already failed. It must be remembered, of course, that not only had enthusiasm cooled through the delay between A.C.D.'s passing and the launching of the Appeal, but that many people had been hit by the world-slump of that year. But though these factors may account for the meagre response, most people in Spiritualism felt sorrowful and a little ashamed, especially when it was recalled that Sir Arthur had spent huge sums to forward the cause.*

A strange feature of some mediumship is a capacity to see into the future. In Minesta's case, this power seems to serve the purpose of preparing her mind, or her receptivity, for whatever may be coming her way. A few examples will serve to illustrate both this power and its purpose. They are taken from the book, *Thy Kingdom Come*, where both the time and the names of those present to corroborate all that happened are given. Sometimes the words quoted were spoken by White Eagle, sometimes by Minesta herself. Thus, on the morning of the day of A.C.D.'s passing a friend of Miss Conan Doyle's was told that the foundations of the bookshop were crumbling (this meant, of course, the Psychic Bookshop at Westminster). As she had not heard how serious was A.C.D.'s illness until she saw the posters announcing his death a few hours later this friend did not realise what was

---

* According to Mr. John Dickson Carr's *Life of Sir Arthur Conan Doyle* the total expended was about £250,000.

meant. It might almost be said that at this time the foundations of Spiritualism itself were crumbling, so grave a blow did A.C.D.'s death prove to the movement; so sad a decline has followed his loss.

Again, Minesta's mind was carefully prepared before the coming of the messenger from France. She was also informed about the existence of the Sages in the Far East, usually referred to by White Eagle as The Brotherhood. This was said on October 30th, 1930, Mr. Bradbrook acting as recorder: ' Again I would stress that the underlying principle on which the work of the Memorial must rest is that this brother's (A.C.D.'s) name must be employed, not for the furtherance of his personality but, as his life was spent, for the establishment of truth and justice. In this manner his name will be used after the death of his body to bring to the Brothers the power they need to build on earth a Temple of the Spirit.' Often so much seems to centre round a man's name and personality, but this particular personality is after all only a means to an end. Realising this, he has already thrown himself into this work with zest and joy because he has been shown its outcome, which will eventually be an earth reborn, a truth set free.

' In this manner the great Brotherhood is already at work. You will soon learn, my friends, that there are those in other parts of the earth to whom the powers and organising ability of the Brotherhood has reached. You will come into contact with another society in France from which you will receive great support.'

These words were spoken nearly four months before Minesta encountered the messenger on the 27th day of January, 1931— January also being a significant month, in that the forces of death or negation end with the old year, and the forces of life or creation arise with the New; so that it was on the ' Master's ' day of that New Year that this work began—for the vibration 9-9-9 is usually considered that of a Master.

On January 9th, 1931, White Eagle said to a group of four friends: ' I am directed to tell you again that the Helper is near. He will be international in his interests and work.'

About ten days later Minesta was asked to arrange for a special meeting on behalf of Lady Conan Doyle and her family, together with a M. Zam Bhotiva who had come from Paris with the sole object of getting into touch with Sir Arthur. As has been said, their meeting was held on January 27th at the W. T. Stead Library in Westminster, the hostess being Miss Estelle Stead, the group consisting of Lady Conan Doyle and her two sons, three friends of the family, the messenger from France, Minesta and her husband. Conditions were not as good as might have been hoped. There was a certain strain, due possibly to the large number of people present, or possibly to the great power which seemed to be focused on the group. Minesta entered, crossed the room and seated herself. At once M. Bhotiva rose and crossed over to her. (Neither had met before.) He said: ' Yes, I know you. We have worked together long long ago—that was in former lives in ancient Egypt. See—I have brought you this little star. It has been sent to you by the Wise Ones for you to wear.' He pinned it onto her dress, made a gesture of blessing and protection, and returned to his seat.

CHAPTER VI

THE 'NINE-NINE-NINE' DAY AND ITS OUTCOME

> 'The work was there and the work was to be done. My own
> personal powers were little enough, but when immortal forces are
> behind you, your real personality counts for nothing.'
>   —Arthur Conan Doyle, *Our American Adventure*.

AT this stage it will be of interest to know what manner of man
this messenger was. He is not easy to describe. Someone who
once met him by appointment at a London tube station during
the rush hour said that he stood out among the crowds like ' an
eagle among pigeons.' This is true, but to say why is not so
easy; he was, perhaps, slightly under average height, about
forty years old, with a mass of hair so dark as to be black, dark
penetrating eyes, strongly-marked features which when he was
touched could soften to an almost Christ-like expression; yet
when he was stirred to anger he looked formidable indeed. His
English was of the sketchiest, so that it needed some concentration
to follow him. Yet such was the power of the man that he
seemed to drive home his meaning—and that meaning was
always something very well worth listening to. In all he was a
man of mystery, an Italian by birth, and had been with the
' Mage' one of the founders of the Polaires. His love and
respect for his chief, the Chevalier Rose-Croix in the East was
profound, and he lived to further his chief's cause and that of
the Polaires. He accorded to White Eagle almost a like respect,
seeming to recognise thus early a wisdom in him and power
of love, which in later years have been made manifest to a great
number of people. M. Bhotiva paid many visits to this country
during the Conan Doyle work, often crossing and arriving in
London without notice by the customary letter or telegram.
Minesta, however, was nearly always aware when he had
reached this country, saying that she could even ' smell' the
particular brand of cigarette he smoked.

What brought him over to Britain in the first place? Here we must turn to a message from their Master which appeared in the *Polaire Bulletin:* ' Arthur Conan Doyle has appeared to us (to the Sages), and among the many interesting things of which he spoke was his decision to interest himself in and help the Polaire Group. Before his death he had promised his friends to give proofs and manifestations of the after life. To-day he let us know, through his communication with the Chevalier Rose-Croix, that he will hold to his promise.

' But not yet: for the spirit of Sir Arthur still waits in his beautiful Scotland for the time of the meeting of the *red* and *violet* rays. This meeting alone will enable him to speak to his friends. Those who would help Sir Arthur should use a dark red light when they meet, and especially on this special day. The medium chosen must carry a six-pointed star to give her the necessary strength.'

When Minesta read this she naturally asked for an explanation. His own particular mission, M. Bhotiva then said, was to help Sir Arthur to give his message and his proof of identity to the world. Before Sir Arthur could speak with knowledge and authority he must be shown, or even traverse, a wide range of the heavenly kingdom. When the average man dies his soul is held within the astral world for a long time, a world which is still close to this world, and is still ' material ' although composed of a finer matter than this. The soul of A.C.D. differed from most souls because it had incarnated under certain ' earth ' rays of great power and significance. No common destiny lay before such a soul once it was able to assert itself. The ' gripping ' power of those rays had remained unbroken by his death; that was why it was necessary, according to instructions received from the Sages, for Minesta and Sir Arthur's family to go to Edinburgh (where A.C.D. was born), to hold there a special meeting on May 22nd, the day of his birth. By this means, in conjunction with the *red* and the *violet* —for which read the rays of the *time* of his birth, and the *place* of his birth—the soul of A.C.D. could be set free from its astral limitations.

M. Bhotiva continued, ' We know Sir Arthur in France.

He loved our country and its people. We too know what manner of man he is. The Polaires call him the "Great Brother" and think of him as such. Nevertheless, no one can escape his destiny, no matter how great, how strong, how good he be. Not even Christ could escape His cross.'

Minesta pondered these matters for a long time afterwards, as well as the fact that M. Bhotiva had said that Sir Arthur earnestly desired to re-state the case for Spiritualism; that he wanted to correct many of the beliefs to which he had formerly subscribed in the light of what he had himself experienced after his passing; and began to realise that this contact of hers with his family, with the Polaires and their messenger, with the Chevalier Rose-Croix on the inner planes, was but the preliminary of a major work to come.

It must be made clear that these talks with M. Bhotiva *followed* the meeting held at the Stead Library on January 27th when he and Minesta first met. This account of that meeting is taken from *Thy Kingdom Come:*

' The group waited until the white light in the small chapel was switched off, the ruby light switched on. The hour which followed stands out and is not lightly to be forgotten. By my side sat the medium, on my left was Miss Estelle Stead; the red glow fell on the earnest and reverent faces around the circle as the guide White Eagle rose. Few can realise without sight or hearing the wonderful transformation and dignity which comes upon his medium, the deep measured voice with which White Eagle speaks, his tenderness and humanity.

' On the table before me is M. Bhotiva's account of what followed, as recorded in the *Polaire Bulletin.* The account reads:

' The meeting was strictly private; the medium was a Mrs. Grace Cooke, well known to English Spiritualists. She wore a silver star, symbol of our fraternity, and the room was lit by a deep red light.

' She went into a trance almost immediately. She then rose, crossed the room, and in a masculine voice recognised by several present as that of her guide, White Eagle, began a long conversation with Lady Doyle and her two sons, Sir Arthur speaking through the mediumship of White Eagle. (On such occasions the guide speaks on behalf of some other spirit, he being the more practised communicator.) We shall not repeat the long conversation which ensued here, for it was strictly personal. After nearly an hour, however, the medium rose again. With closed eyes and a firm step she approached Zam Bhotiva (Z.B. writes of himself in the third person) saying, " There is a gentleman here whom I have not known during my earth life, but with whom I am now linked in view of a common work."

' The medium stopped in front of our brother, held out her hand and a joyful, manly " I am glad to meet you " rang through the room. A long and low pitched conversation then took place between the " dead " and the " living." Conan Doyle made himself known to Zam Bhotiva as " brother," and then, turning again to those present, proceeded to speak of the Polaires as " a group destined to help in the moulding of the future of the world. . . . For the times are near." He then said, turning again to Zam Bhotiva, "I must speak with you again in six days' time. I have some important matters to communicate to you. The work, to which I can set no limit, begins."

' It was thus that a man whom the world calls " dead " made an appointment with Zam Bhotiva.'

When Minesta returned home on that night she felt somewhat disturbed on account of the unusual nature of what had happened. She then received the following instruction from White Eagle: ' This man (Zam Bhotiva) has an important part to play. He is our servant. No harm will come if you give yourself to our work. Great effects will eventually result from this first contact, and these will be widely felt and will presently shatter the doubts of the many who cannot believe in the life of the spirit. As yet there are many conflicting interests which may hinder the work. *This messenger is sent because of instructions from Tibet, and he who sent the message knows of you from there.'*

The account of the second meeting with the Messenger six days later is again from the *Polaire Bulletin*. The group consisted of four people.

' The guide of the medium again takes control and speaks in

the same manly voice. The room is lighted with a deep red light, and the medium wears the tiny six-pointed star.

'*White Eagle:* "I speak of one whom I shall call 'Nobleheart'" (as has been said, White Eagle often bestows a name indicative of the character or soul of the person concerned), "known to you as Arthur Conan Doyle. He now recognises that his passing was for a far greater purpose than the ordinary mind can realise. He is to be used to bring to the earth *fresh truths* and light. Instructions were sent to Paris to this brother (Z.B.) so that he might be directed to the medium through whom he could speak . . . Conan Doyle holds out his hand to you' (to Z.B.) 'in brotherly love. He is ready to help your Brotherhood. His name is a power in this country: if it be a power for good take and use it for good."

The report goes on: 'Another communicator takes the place of White Eagle. The voice changes (it would appear that Z.B. now believed the speaker to be no other than the Chevalier Sage, but hesitates to say so directly). "Conan Doyle and the Wise Knight are now in harmony; in harmony and brotherly love. Conan Doyle is a great spirit now released from the flesh, and so will be able to serve in *all* spheres of life. Reach to his soul if you would contact his true spirit. Only in the impersonal spiritual power can you receive divine inspiration to forward your work; and indeed the personal must become divine.

'"See—the star rises in the East—it is the sign of the Polaires, the sign of the two equilateral triangles!"' Then followed details about the "years of fire" or disasters drawing near to mankind, details which are withheld, coupled with an appeal for friendship between France and Britain for "the link is now made."

The account continues : 'We do not comment on these two meetings. The Polaires hold no dogmas, but have a deep respect for all the faiths and beliefs of man. We have summarised and have reported as faithfully as possible the two meetings which took place, and can only say that according to the communications of the Sages received through the Oracle of the Force Astrale, Sir Arthur spoke to us through the mediumship of White Eagle.

' Regarding these meetings it must be distinctly understood at the outset that neither the medium nor her husband knew anything about the Polaire organisation, nor of what it sought to accomplish in London. We went to London to obtain certain definite evidence, and employed every safeguard to guarantee that evidence. Moreover, the Wise Ones informed us that at the end of the second meeting the medium would give direct proof that she was in communication with our Chiefs. When she awoke from trance she told M. Bhotiva that she saw a lofty mountain and a man with a luminous dark face who held out to her a six-pointed star. Here was the proof for which we had waited.'

Here ends the Polaire account of what must have been a notable display of knowledge on the part of White Eagle, such knowledge being entirely unknown to the medium and her husband, who had acted as recorder during the two meetings.

Together with this account of the meeting of Z.B. with Sir Arthur Conan Doyle a facsimile of a letter from Lady Conan Doyle appeared in the *Bulletin des Polaires*. Even after the lapse of years it is worth reproducing this letter, not only because of its intrinsic interest but because it affirms the recognition of Sir Arthur as the communicator by the one person whose confirmation was most valuable and who could speak with the most authority.

Another factor which increased the bewilderment of these two was that, unknown to themselves, they were being brought under the ray or projection of a special Polaire group in Paris which had been detailed to help A.C.D. in his mission. This group sat for months at regular intervals to project a ray illuminating both Sir Arthur and his medium. It must always be understood that in their work the Polaires were forbidden by their Chiefs to constrain or overrule the freewill of any man. They must not attempt to dominate, impose or influence anyone to adopt or follow any particular line of conduct, however admirable it might seem to other people. To *illumine* a soul—for this Brotherhood was working with its own soul-power and not with minds or bodies—and thereby to help it to recognise and follow

TELEGRAMS:
Crowborough.
Tel. No. 77.

Feb. 3rd

WINDLESHAM,
CROWBOROUGH,
SUSSEX.

Dear Monsieur Bothiva

I am writing to say
that I am so glad that
at the Seance held in
London on Tuesday 27th Jny
husband came through & spoke
to you unexpectedly about
Les Polaires Brotherhood.

With kind regards

Yours sincerely

Jean Conan Doyle

[Reproduced from the 'Bulletin des Polaires' for 9th February 1931]

LETTER FROM LADY CONAN DOYLE TO M. ZAM BHOTIVA, FEBRUARY 3RD, 1931 the light within itself was to practise a white magic; to attempt in any way to overrule the volition of that soul was a form of black magic bearing terrible penalties in this life and the next. No pains were spared to make this crystal-clear to every Polaire. May it be as plainly expressed in this book.

Only the recipients of this ray of illumination are in a position to testify to its reality and power. Here Minesta and her husband were in a peculiarly favourable position, since both now wore the little Polaire star which formed a link or point of contact, and both were sensitive enough to be receptive to the Polaire ray. It is no easy matter to describe their reactions. We have all seen an actor on a darkened stage picked out by a spotlight. That is how it felt to these two. They were picked out; something was reaching them, something which was affecting them during the weeks and months that followed, and which was greatly helpful in its influence.

Some readers will doubtless want to know why such an advanced soul as that of A.C.D. should suffer any limitation after death. They will argue that his years of devotion to good causes, his stalwart championship of right against wrong on all possible occasions, his sacrifice of income, time, strength and even life itself in the cause of Spiritualism, should have set him free.

Yes, this is a sound argument. But here is another line of thought; most of us can presumably do one or two things pretty well either with hands or head or even with both. The achievement of most of us is small. Indeed, how many of us can *excel* at any one separate thing? Very few; but here and there someone achieves it. This does not necessarily refer to a spiritual genius such as a Jesus, but to some ordinary man, living in our midst, immersed in the daily round and common task, but doing everything better than other people. One has to read more than one biography of the man Doyle to gain appreciation of all that he was and did. In almost everything he touched, no matter whether he followed a beaten trail or became a pioneer (as with the Sherlock Holmes saga, or with a new sport such as ski-ing), he excelled. If his physical size was phenomenal, so was the scope of his interests and accomplishments.

Now it so happens that man can only excel when he devotedly and passionately desires to do so. To excel at many things— sports, writing books, or crusading in this, that or the other direction on behalf of many a cause—a passion of devotion must be given to all. This means that the soul of the doer is bound up with all that it does. If the inclination of its interests is heavenly, it becomes a saint or seer; if earthly, then it ties itself down to earth. Some folk live out their lives only a quarter or a half conscious, so that many valuable and interesting things escape their notice. Rarely does one meet anyone one-hundred-per-cent alive with fire and energy. This may arise because, as occultists say, the majority of us do not incarnate in full. A portion of our soul stays behind in the invisible world from which we come, to call us back again home when we lay down our burden here at death; so that anyone who incarnates *his whole self* has some difficulty at first in breaking his earthly ties when his time comes. This is as it may be. What this line of thought may make clear is that if A.C.D. was one of these then his service to Spiritualism, noble and selfless as it was, did not differ largely from his other material interests. His task was always to try to convince hard-headed worldly people of the reality of survival by producing substantial evidence of an after life. He largely devoted himself to the search for such evidence rather than to the spiritual and religious significance of these matters, so that even his Spiritualism in some degree ranked among his material interests.

CHAPTER VII

'MORE BEAUTIFUL THAN HE HAD EVER CONCEIVED'

' This world is but the ante-chamber of the next.
—The Bishop in *Sir Nigel*.

AFTER a further sitting on February 2nd it became clear that little more could be done to help this soul, which (as White Eagle said) had been *captured* at birth by the earth rays, until May 22nd following. The missioner was not yet ready to commence his mission. The little group of people selected to receive his message were still in process of being attuned by the ray from the Wise Knight, passed on through the projection of the Polaire group in Paris; during the many months that followed they were always conscious of that ray, linking them with affection and sympathy to A.C.D. and with respect and devotion to the Wise Knight.

What came next? A series of preliminary sittings were held in a little upper room furnished as a chapel in the home of Minesta. Here is the record of the first, on February 20th, 1931, M. Bhotiva being present.*

White Eagle: ' You are right; a certain time must elapse before A.C.D. is ready to begin his appointed work. But the day draws near when the two forces, the red and the blue rays (those of the *time* and the *place* of the birth of A.C.D.) will contact. Then you will get close to Arthur Conan Doyle. He wants you all to know that he is waiting (oh, how eagerly !) to throw all his power of service into the new work which has been revealed to him . . . On this little group is concentrated the ray of a great six-pointed star, and there is a great white " House " out in the east from which comes a brilliant beam of light right into this

---

* It should be again noted that all these early records are greatly abbreviated.

chapel. Now I can see writing. Something will come which has to be put into a book which will be printed in both English and French. This writing will come from (be originated or influenced by?) the Wise Knight. Minesta knows nothing about this (we had then, of course, no thought about these matters ever going into print).'

Here is an extract from the next record—again taken from the book, *Thy Kingdom Come:*

' So strange and wonderful has been the hour spent in that little upper room that its memory can never be erased. As I write again the glow of the red lamp falls on the gracious presence of Lady Conan Doyle; on Denis, as big a man as his father but as dark and " southern " in appearance as was his father fair and of the North; on Mary Conan Doyle; on Z.B. and on Mrs. Caird's head bent over the table as her scurrying pencil strives to keep pace with the spoken words.

' Beside me sits Minesta, eyes closed in deep trance, previously so feminine in every aspect; now to look away one forgets her womanhood almost at once. White Eagle is speaking, and he supplements his words with gestures which lend them point and urgency, and this as gracefully as bends a silver birch tree to the breeze. He prays to the " Great White Spirit," Source of all things, for His blessing and presence in our midst; then continues:

' " White Eagle greets all his friends (W.E. usually speaks of himself in the third person, seeming to dislike the conventional " I "). He is now a spokesman *only* for those who come here to serve. The number six is given (to Z.B.). Now the Wise Knight comes to greet you, my son; you know him? He brings Arthur Conan Doyle with him. He would have White Eagle say to those here who already love, or will come to love the soul and personality of Arthur, that he (the Wise Knight) would have them know that he also would serve both him and you. I also am the servant of the Wise Knight.

' " He would have you know that this is a greater soul than even those who know him best have realised, and has yet a noble mission to perform. Indeed his mission is more vital than anything he has yet accomplished. He calls to you, who are already dear to him, to help him in his service.

' " He still loves the cause of Spiritualism. His whole desire was ever to give comfort to hearts which were aching and broken by the stress of life. That is why he crossed and recrossed the world to bring hope and consolation to the bereaved and sorrowful. Now that he is released from his fleshly bondage—yet still limited by certain astral ties—his one desire is to press forward.

' " He sends his love, deep and sincere, to his beloved family. He must have a clear channel and only a clear channel through which to work, without any conflicting interests—for when he is free he will come with great power. No one will doubt him when once he comes into full possession of his power; no one will doubt. For this is no mediocre soul, and only through the purest channel will he manifest. Be assured that this is no longer a personal matter. In essence it is universal.

' " Sorrowfully we say again that there comes great suffering to humanity. Mankind is working up to a catastrophe. This man realised something of this truth previously (after the first world war), when bereaved humanity most needed help; now also he is being prepared, and is preparing himself to give to man a clearer statement concerning the conditions he will encounter when he enters the life after death. He spent the latter part of his life in teaching the people what they might expect from an *earthly* standpoint. Soon he will speak with the authority of his own experience of the life beyond. All your doubts will be set at rest. The manifestations will come, so be prepared. In the meantime wait quietly as he would have you, and all will be made clear.

' " A.C.D. now finds that a different condition of spiritual understanding is coming to him, for he is reacting to wonderful revelations which to him appear far more beautiful than anything he had ever conceived, dreamt of, or been given to understand. These conditions are no longer personal but universal, and this you must try to grasp.

' " The Wise Knight comes again in his shining raiment, to

show us again the star of six points, and to speak of numbers —of the three—six—nine; He shows us the red cross and the heart of a rose (the Rosicrucian symbol) and says, " *Let your light so shine before men!* " Oh, this light is the greatest thing which has ever dawned on man! There will come to you, my brothers and sisters, the great One himself in his human body . . . some day. (Some of the Masters have power to manifest in this way, the " Wise Knight " among them.)

' " It is all to be simple, this revelation; it will not be beyond the capacity of anyone to understand. The problem rather is so to put it into words as to make it *real*. For this revelation will not be about some distant heaven beyond man's comprehension, but concerns a new dawning of understanding right within man's own soul, a spiritual comprehension which cannot separate him from anyone whom he loves who has passed on, but bring only a stronger link, a closer bond.

' " You must all realise by now the power and the love which surrounds you, and also the truth and sincerity of the purpose behind. You have been told of big happenings which are approaching. How little does this express the shattering which the world will someday receive! This is where the messages of A.C.D. will someday come into their own. At present the time is not ripe for this, but in due course they will sweep aside all doubt in the minds of men.'

' (*To M. Bhotiva.*) " You are aware that our brother Arthur is now closely linked with the Great Ones? You know that he waits to be enabled with the aid of his friends to give that clear account of the life beyond death and that you must hold a special meeting for that purpose? Good.

' " Remember, it must be held on a " two-two " day (on the twenty-second of May, his birthday) because his spirit was captured a long time ago by earth on a " two-two " day, and on a " two-two " day must be set free—as a bird is freed, without trammels or hampering. Up to the present A.C.D. has been only able to get through " little bits," but what he has to say will presently come with such fullness and power that your hearts will be overjoyed.

' " I now show you a symbol—I want to build on a Square of Four for the future work. You will find that the revelation which has been promised will deal not only with the life-beyond-death but with the coming of the Christ Spirit; and this in years to come will bring a very definite change, a revival of the spirit in men's thoughts and literature. So also will the governments of the nations be someday directed from the Spirit. The curtain which now shrouds men and women from the truth, from the incoming light, will be rent; and illumination will dawn so brightly that men will see differently, will see truth truly. . . .

' " That is enough.

' " Reflect well. I cannot impress you sufficiently with the significance of the words spoken tonight.' "

The idea of building on a Square of Four will be familiar to all Freemasons. It so happened that all the sitters (Minesta and Mrs. Caird included) were Masons, as was A.C.D. It also happened that the group finally decided that four members made the ideal number, members of the Conan Doyle family and M. Bhotiva being only occasional visitors.

One more significant incident to close this chapter. In the month of April, 1931, a photograph was published in the London *News Chronicle* of a message written on a photographic plate in Sir Arthur's own unmistakable handwriting and signed by himself. It read:

' *My dear all of you. I have greatly looked forward to this, but I cannot come in contact as I ought. There lies my difficulty. My greetings to you all. You are indeed doing God's work.*

Arthur Conan Doyle.'

This photograph was obtained through the mediumship of Mr. William Hope of Crewe, a most trustworthy photographic medium, who obtained many of his results by merely holding an unopened packet of photographic plates between his hands; or else by exposing in his camera a marked plate which had been taken from a new packet by someone who had marked it and who oversaw everything which subsequently happened to that plate, so that there was no possibility of mistake or fraud. What lends this incident value is that it provides a completely independent proof or corroboration of the message of the Force Astrale, ' *I cannot come in contact as I ought. There lies my difficulty.*' These words substantiate the Polaire message.

CHAPTER VIII

THE NEW MAN IN A RENEWED WORLD

'Light, especially the celestial light (and this is to be well noted) must not be suddenly presented in its full radiance (lest we be completely blinded and hardened in our ignorance) but gradually introduced. For men must be raised by slow stages. . . . We must make a beginning with the things which they know, and slowly lead them to what they do not know.'

Kominsky in *The Way of Light.*

WHEN this fateful meeting took place on May 22nd, 1931, Minesta had been on the Spiritualist platform for some eighteen years. Not every exponent of Spiritualism stays the course so long. By then she was a superb natural clairvoyant, whose messages from and descriptions of people in the spirit world went home with hardly an exception. For years, as has been said, she had been working in Spiritualist Churches, a heavy task and duty taken in conjunction with the claims of home and family. Having become so immersed in the movement, she had little time for matters outside her home and work. Her interest in, say, Theosophy and occultism, for example, was only tepid, she having commenced one or two books on these subjects and laid them aside. Much the same applied—must it be confessed ?— to the writings of Arthur Conan Doyle, of which she had read one book only. We have therefore to see her in our mind's eye as a person making use to the full extent of her strength and the special powers with which she had been endowed, in the belief that her most important mission was to succour the bereaved and comfort the heavy-hearted. She did this through Spiritualism, which at that time (it must be remembered) was a progressive and lively movement, getting a considerable and not always unsympathetic publicity in the press, and claiming as advocates a host of men and women prominent in science, on the stage, in literature, at the bar, and in many other walks of life. Having no knowledge of occultism or Theosophy or their literature, her own mind could not intrude on the communications which were to come; the channel prepared for A.C.D.'s message was, therefore, free from preconceived ideas. This, being important, should be borne in mind by the reader, as should another important matter, this being how strongly the mind and personality of A.C.D. came through in his written work, and in his public speaking. The generation in which his name was a household word is passing and a succeeding generation may be unfamiliar with his charm of style and expression. The present writer always found this magical—magical is not too strong a word. Conan Doyle always wrote in plain English, the plainer and simpler the better, making no use of sharply novel or emphatic words or phrasing in order to jolt his reader to attention (as did say, Robert Louis Stevenson). He had no need; subtly (or magically) his writing reached out and won attention with his first sentence and held it to the end. How this came about is difficult to define, but certainly it succeeded. Perhaps it was because the nature of the man himself permeated his writing in no common degree. The love of romance in him held us until the book ended. He was someone, we felt as we read on, patently sincere and honest whom it would be good to know because we felt we wanted to know him; we gladly made his acquaintance through his books, finding there a sturdy good sense and right feeling which again was good to encounter; and lastly we felt he was British through and through with the best of Britain, and so his books came as a breath of home. These are some of the reasons why the word ' magical ' was made use of in the first place.

Why is all this written after this lapse of time? Because when *Thy Kingdom Come* was first published, everyone was familiar with the Conan Doyle books and with their author. As has been said, his was a peculiarly individual style—or rather, the man vested his style with his own individuality; therefore when *Thy Kingdom Come* was published it went out to readers long familiar with that style and therefore able to say whether or not his messages read like messages coming from Conan Doyle. It was therefore important that they should have come through a medium unfamiliar with the Conan Doyle style of writing (as they did) and in a deep trance state where she remembered nothing afterwards of what had transpired.

This being so, was that channel translucent enough, pure enough for not only the message but something of the style, character and personality of A.C.D. to come though unimpaired? Yes; it would seem so. *Thy Kingdom Come* was read by many thousands of people. Not one of these readers ever wrote afterwards to say that they did not believe that it was Conan Doyle communicating; not one of them challenged it; the book won acceptance (albeit mostly a silent acceptance) everywhere, for it had such a power in it that twenty years afterwards people are still searching for secondhand copies.

A later message through the Force Astrale somewhat altered the plan for May 22nd, as it had been found impractical to transport so large a party to Edinburgh for this one meeting. Instead, it was arranged for it to take place at a large country house near Bletchley in Buckinghamshire, to which Minesta journeyed early on the morning of the day appointed, and spent hours of quiet preparation for and dedication to her task among gardens and fields luxuriant with the spring. As the link with Edinburgh was still necessary it was arranged that three friends would sit in that city, tuning in with the group at Bletchley; while a large group of Polaire Brothers met to project their ray from Paris direct to the group at the time fixed. Perhaps only Minesta was aware how great an ordeal was this meeting, for she felt that everyone's hopes and expectations centred and depended on herself; on her poise, her stability and quietness of mind and spirit, her strength and courage; as indeed it did. Nor did it help when those who were to sit in the group seemed strained and over-anxious when the cars drove up, the first bringing Mrs. Caird, M. Bhotiva, and the Chief of the Polaires, Monsieur R. Odin (who had come from France for this sole purpose). Shortly afterwards came Lady Doyle, her sons Adrian and Denis, and Mr. Bradbrook. To the latter we owe our record of what transpired.

At the appointed time the group met. Here is the scene as described by Mr. Bradbrook:

' A beautiful room—a group of delicately tinted tulips catch the glow of a crimson-shaded table lamp; a similar lamp diffuses subdued illumination upon the open piano. The embers of a fire complete the effect; a faint fragrance comes from an indistinct mass of mauve which proved to be lilac blossoms.

' Silently and unobtrusively the seats are filled. Three figures seem to dominate; two are the Polaire Brothers wearing the blue robes of their order, the other a figure in a dress of deep blue. The notes of a largo fall on our ears. . . . We enter the Silence.

' The figure in blue rises to her feet to pray: " Great White Spirit, full of faithfulness we come. May Thy power dominate all creatures; may humanity be illumined by the glory of Thy light. May these Thy servants who bow before Thee become so filled with truth that they give light to the world of men. May Thy Light ever guide them on the path. Amen."

'*White Eagle speaks:* "There are great presences with you at this special time. The Wise Knight is here, and sends the light of his power and presence through White Eagle. Arthur Conan Doyle, whom we call ' Nobleheart' in the world of spirit (for this is how we regard him) is so happy to come. He means to speak personally to you today, so he asks that every heart here will be filled with tender love for him, for this alone can help him. Keep silent in mind and heart and let him speak. He is closer to you in spirit than you can ever realise; closer now than ever he was in the body but in a different way. It is difficult for us to explain, for spiritual truths are hard to put into words. Can you understand when we say that he has become *united* to your spirit? Your hearts and not your minds must interpret his message. Presently you will know and understand what he means."

' Minesta lies back in her chair, completely relaxed. White Eagle has gone. Now there comes a change over her. When she speaks the voice is different, though still masculine in timbre. Her face has fallen into other lines. The gestures which White

Eagle used were fluent and wonderfully expressive; now they are few and clumsy, as of one too reserved to make open gestures. The very phrasing is changed, it is that of one with mastery over words. Neither is the speech broken or sentences clipped, as it was with White Eagle. There has come the burr of a northerner. . . . It is the voice of one from far places, broken and amazed, but gradually gaining in power.

' " Yes . . . yes . . . yes. I am coming—I am coming . . . Yes . . . *Thank God!* What a gathering ! " (The speaker seemed to see or realise the presence of some concourse of Beings of brightness and splendour unseen by the people present). " I seem to be among a great company of friends. . . . The Light is very bright; this is grand, grand . . . Speak . . . Speak to me ! " (A murmur of voices: " We welcome you.")

' " Arthur speaks to you again—my wife ! " (Here a portion of the record is omitted.)

' " Thank God ! God bless you ! I am here—I am here ! You must forgive my emotion. It is not like me to feel emotion, but it is so marvellous to speak with you all again. You do not, you cannot, understand what all this means. *I have come back!* . . . Yes, it is all coming to me now. I have spoken, of course I have spoken before, but not with power. I have passed through some wonderful experiences—I want to tell you, I want to tell you all about them. It is difficult—yes, I have heard you calling me. At such times I have been close, and yet there has been some barrier. Now at last I have been given power. But I must keep calm, for I have a definite message to give, my friends. Will you therefore follow what I say with close attention?

' " I would thank all those who have helped me. . . . I seemed to be very puzzled when I first realised where I was. My one desire was to get back then—and then . . . oh, there is so much to explain, so much to tell you. I have been to my home, I have been *in* my home, I have seen my dear ones. What is it which has prevented me from doing all that I intended ? . . . I see a mission before me. I have to give a message to you all. . . . It is difficult." '

' The figure of Minesta lay back apparently completely

exhausted. For a while it seemed the speaker had lost his control. With growing apprehension the group watched her. Was this the end? The minutes slipped away—five—ten—fifteen. When the voice spoke again there was more than a timbre of White Eagle in the speech, as if he also was supporting the medium. Presently the voice gained confidence.

' " I am still here, gathering power so that I can speak with you further. No, I have not left you, but I got confused—although I have learned a considerable amount about the process of manifestation from the other side of life. Much that is erroneous must be cleared away. I see now that there is a part of me which can manifest to a slight degree in various places and under various conditions. I see now that some of the phenomena of Spiritualism are attributable to astral projection and astral memories. Thus it is possible for a sensitive or medium to pick up these astral memories which have been registered in certain places and conditions of thought, and which can be represented to the people of earth as coming from a spirit being. There have already been a variety of communications of this sort as from myself, but not always projected consciously from me. I so desire to clear up this point.★

' " I have passed through what you know as the astral life, and have now been cleared from the conditions which were hampering my work. To clear a soul of the astral vibrations is not altogether an easy matter; but do not be misguided with regard to this state; it is a necessary evil. To be freed from these astral ties does not sever a man from those he loves, but it sets free his spirit and allows him to enter into the full realisation of his own nature.

' " You do not know the true selves of one another as you will when you pass into the illimitable consciousness of God; and the same material ties which bind you down here to the earth will still bind your soul when you leave the earth-condition, until you wake to the glory of God's love.

★ This perhaps refers to the many communications claiming to come from A.C.D. which the post brought almost daily to Lady Conan Doyle at that time.

' " By this we mean a loosening of the *personal* and an entering into the *impersonal* consciousness of the creative Essence which man calls God; and in that consciousness a realisation of the " perfectness " of all those you love.

' " I must work. I must go forward. The mission which we have to fulfil is now shown to me. I see so clearly now, whereas before I saw as in a glass darkly. Now I see you and all men face to face. Most of all I see *myself.*

' " I thank God for the many opportunities He gave me to help my fellow men.

' " I see certain things in which I was mistaken. No man can have the entire truth. In some respects I was misled. Before my passing I had had some suspicions regarding astral memories, and was aware that certain spiritualistic phenomena were attributable to these memories. But I did not believe that *all* such communications arose from this cause; nor do they! I tell you definitely that it is possible for the human spirit, which is the real man—if that man has a definite mission to perform for the good of humanity—to come back to execute it and so help forward the evolution of the race.

' " Survival of the human soul is a proven fact, is unquestionable. But the world is waiting for a greater demonstration and a more evident proof of this mighty truth. Humanity must realise that communication with astral memories left behind by a soul after its passing and with the real spirit of a man are vastly different. Before any true communication can take place it is necessary for *the spirit of the person left behind on earth* to be raised to the *consciousness of spiritual reality.* This is why so much is futile in the spiritualistic movement today; but the glorious truth of survival must be given to humanity in clear and perfect form.

' " *Personal responsibility and the redeeming power of love:* these are the great things. A man's personal responsibility is an irrefutable fact; for I find that it is not only a man's *actions* in the outer world which count, but his *inmost thought.* This is because the spirit world to which he will go is a world of thought, his own thought, *an internal state* rather than an *external condition* in which he lives. Thought promotes action; the actions of each man again promote thought in his fellows; and we thereby return again to the thought world. Truly is it said that as a man sows he shall surely reap.

' " In a broad sense the seeds of thought that he sows are interpreted as actions; but now I find that thought is more powerful than action, since one of the first things a man is faced with on his escape from earth life is *a world of his own thought*.

' " Let us pass on from this condition to the next; but not forgetting that it is not always pleasant to be isolated *in a world which represents all the thoughts one has projected during a lifetime*. But God is Love, Wisdom and Justice. I would not have it otherwise, for it has been revealed to me in a most marvellous way how the love of God can manifest in the deepest heart of His children.

' " *Personal responsibility and the redeeming power of love*—this one great lesson I have learned, and pass it on to all of you. No man can really live or die apart from God . . . God—Christ —Love—call it what you will. The men of earth have seen a supreme manifestation of that great power of Love, expressed in One—no, in several personalities."

' A long pause ensued. The speaker had been under deep emotion and agitation throughout, and his power was now obviously flagging. He continued, " Yes—yes—yes. The redeeming power of Love is supreme. I must conclude my message with this. Love! Not personal love . . . impersonal . . . love for all men. Now I see the great need of all men— yes, the Master."

' *White Eagle interposes:* " I think we can help now, as our brother is not able to finish. White Eagle speaks. This is Arthur's birthday, his ' second ' birthday, and from now on he gathers an ever-increasing power. Vibrations are very strong and he is overjoyed, although he says, " Nonsense; I did not lose my head!" But when you are dealing with conditions which are entirely unusual you will understand that these things happen. He is so full of enthusiasm and desire to serve, to work, to fight on and to win. He does so want it ' all on the level.' He is sensible of your token of love and remembrance to his old body (this probably refers to flowers laid that morning on his grave). He is much more satisfied with the new. I am to say that he gets younger and has now a new body strong and ' full of beans,' he says.

' " What follows now you may think peculiar, but he was very fond of the living creatures in the woods and gardens around his old home, and of a pet squirrel. He still loves to come and watch its little ways, and is still friendly with it. His was always a heart full of love for the ' little people '—so boyish, so simple, so big, honest and sincere with its desire to help. His one desire was to give proof and comfort to the broken-hearted. There is one more thing he wanted to say (he stands on my left amid a group of shining forms most beautiful to behold), and that was about the many prophecies of catastrophes to come which he received a year or two before his passing. He says, ' Do you not see how linked up we are already with the New Age? We have before us a mighty work. There must be a great effort put forward to help humanity in its crisis. We must therefore spread the truth, and in that way make preparation so that souls do not come over here to dwell in darkness and then fall back into—no, he will not complete that sentence. . . ." '

A brief *blessing* or *benediction* completes the record of that day, spoken under conditions of extreme emotional strain. Already we see that the dominant urge of A.C.D.—beyond even that of family and affection—was this imperative message waiting to be delivered, this mission to which all else must be subordinated.

A.C.D. managed to strike a keynote. He laid, as it were, a foundation on which all that followed was to be built when he used the words, ' *As a man sows so he must surely reap.*' To this he added, ' In a broad sense the seeds of thought that he sows are interpreted as actions; but now I find that *thought* is more powerful than *action*, since one of the first things a man is faced with on his escape from earth life is *a world of his own thought.*'

CHAPTER IX

DEFINITIONS; AND THE 'MATERIAL PROOF'

' Open to all be the Gates of Deathlessness.'
—The Buddha.

It seems necessary here to break the continuity of A.C.D.'s message in order to define one or more of the terms employed, such as ' soul ' or the ' astral world.' For what does the word ' soul ' mean? It means *ourself*; that is, man's inner self apart from the body physical that we drag around, which demands nearly all our strength, time and energy to nourish, clothe, house, protect, transport from place to place, amuse and exercise; and eight hours' sleep in order to rest it every night. The soul is *ourself*. We are apart from our body only when we are carried away from it by something which absorbs us—by music, poetry, flowers or scenery, by drama or the ballet, by deep meditation, aspiration or spiritual illumination. Then do we function in our soul. We *are* that soul in all the higher reaches of our being, and our memories, interests, enthusiasms, thoughts, feelings, aspirations comprise it. Sometimes we are all soul-ful; but oftener when the body is sick, sorry and complaining, we are mostly body. Nevertheless, our soul is ourselves as we really are, and as we shall be after the death of the body when we shall first migrate to astral realms.

Not that there will be anything very novel in our astral environment, since we go there every night when we fall asleep. Sleep being a little death, we are well practised in dying, and in this fashion die three hundred and sixty-five times yearly. With each new day we awake. With the same certainty we shall presently awake after death, since both sleeping and dying are natural functions of our being.

Why then do we not remember anything about the astral places which we are said to visit during sleep? But we do, though we store our knowledge in a different compartment—or department—of ourselves, away from the self of every day. We are often ignorant of the extent of our ignorance. We know hardly anything, for example, about this physical body. We don't know whether physical matter is real, or what electricity really is. (The two may be very closely linked—who knows?) We don't even know what our world looks like, because our physical senses have so narrow a range that there are colours we cannot see, sounds we cannot hear, scents we do not register. This being so, man has a distorted and incorrect impression of the world in which he lives. We are, however, *aware* that everything in it is in a state of vibration, and that we ourselves vibrate in accord with a host of other vibrations. This we believe and accept scientifically. We need therefore only one step further to believe that there are other vibrations around us, not necessarily physical but ethereal or astral.

There are indeed astral worlds encompassing this, each in a differing state of vibration from coarser to finer. ' Encompassing ' is the word, for they are not distant planets like Mars or Venus, but are additional departments or colonies of this world, which they encase—much as an onion is encased by its various ' skins '; and yet also interpenetrate our world with themselves, much as water soaks through a sponge.

These astral worlds are mostly of a higher vibration than the physical, and therefore consist of a finer matter. Human life is less burdened since the astral body worn over there by man does not weigh down its wearer, but is a thing of beauty, health and joy. This is the Summerland beloved by Spiritualists. Souls go there (souls being humans freed from the flesh but otherwise unchanged) and inhabit an astral body. They do not at once become greatly wise or spiritual. Rest and refreshment after the toils of their earth life is the first necessity. This they obtain, and they remain in the astral world while time slips past.

Some will say this is too *good* to be true. Nothing is too good to be true. Therefore it is perhaps a pity wilfully to believe, habitually to believe, in things too *bad* to be true, of which there are many varieties, most of which are only bogies. But if people find this makes them happy—well, why not? What matters to us is that the astral worlds are very close to us always; because they interpenetrate our world and even influence our daily life, whether we are conscious or unconscious of the fact.

Because these worlds are so close, the majority of spiritualistic contacts are with people of the astral, who are little changed from their former selves, except that their life is more serene than ours, less limited, less burdened, and their world more beautiful. They are not greatly wise, and their message lacks power. Great things are not demanded of those living in the restful Summerland.

There is, unfortunately, another side to the picture. We have considered the higher astral worlds (or planes, to be more accurate). But what of those of a slower, of a lower vibration; perhaps even lower than this earth? These are not pleasant places, for they are peopled by humans whose lives have attuned them to such planes. They are grey, misty, dark-November-fog places, good to get out of. That is why they exist; to spur their folk to get away, by their own spiritual efforts. Some are worse even than the November-fog plane, but it does no good to try to frighten people into goodness. The Church tried out this method for centuries without success. Hence the decline in the popularity of hell-fire preaching.

Whither is all this leading us? To a better understanding of the 'birthday' message of A.C.D., when he said that 'to be cleared from astral ties was not altogether an easy matter.' This was surely an understatement when it meant so great an act, so great a surrender, on his part. For at that moment he must have relinquished his promised Summerland of rest, refreshment and recreation which was his due after his strenuous years. Yet, in the Summerland life there is an element of forgetfulness, even of heedlessness of the cry of pain rising from men—that 'cry which hath no language but a cry!' For A.C.D. there could be no forgetfulness, no laying down of his burden, no sealing of the heart. A new dedication, a new crusade was waiting to establish a new truth since the earlier truth for which he had formerly laboured proved insufficient.

Therefore he said: ' In a broad sense the *seeds* of thought that he (man) sows are interpreted as *actions:* but now I find that thought is more powerful than action, since one of the first things a man is faced with on his escape from earth life is *a world of his own thought.*'

Consider these words in the light of what has been written about the astral planes, whereon man prepares for himself an abiding place by his own thought and feeling during his years on earth. He migrates to a world of his own thought, a self-constructed home or environment. One is reminded of the saying in the Bible, to the effect that *whatsoever* (sins or blessing ?) *a man binds to himself on earth shall be bound to him in heaven; and whatsoever he shall loose from himself on earth shall be loosed from him in heaven.* Here the same truth is conveyed again. To the world of our own thought which we go to inhabit, our sins and shortcomings will be grafted, but also the goodness that we do.

It must be realised that this A.C.D. communication was coming to us, not from an astral world of people like ourselves, but from a source wiser, higher, purer, with a message far more powerful and enduring. This being so, what of the medium or instrument through which the message was to come? Surely the transmission of this message entailed some pains? Indeed, yes; for Minesta had to forego much. It is true that the power and light of the Wise Knight made this contact possible, and was continually sustaining her. But that contact was a continually shattering experience. After the Bletchley meeting she was exhausted for some days. What intensified the problem was that she was pledged to speak at or work for numerous Spiritualistic centres, and the alternation between the astral contacts of the latter and with A.C.D. meant the eventual abandonment of her work for organised Spiritualism—one hesitates to say ' orthodox ' Spiritualism, but it is the more accurate designation.

After the meeting of the 22nd, the Polaires returned to France, and the other sitters to their homes. The task of obtaining the A.C.D. message now rested with Minesta and her three helpers —that is, with the ' Square of Four ' anticipated by White Eagle.

On the whole we shall find this ' Square ' proved steady at its task during many months to come.

*   *   *

Those who know White Eagle best are aware that he never comes without prayer, that he is always composed and leisurely, always dignified and serene. ' Why hurry,' he says on occasion, ' when you have all eternity before you? ' Perhaps this is why nobody has ever seen him ruffled, hasty or irritable, or heard him speak ill of any man. Only kind words pass his lips.

This being so, the impetuosity with which A.C.D. jumped in in his haste to convince us that none other than he had spoken on May 22nd, was surprising as was the assertion that he had been trying for days to get this confirmation through; he managed also to confirm the salient points of his message of the 22nd, although White Eagle had to help him time and again. It was obvious that A.C.D. had much to learn before delivering his message, and that contrary to Spiritualistic beliefs communication between the worlds was proving a matter of much difficulty.

Nearly a month had passed since the last meeting.

A.C.D.: ' I have been trying for days to come through. Now let me thank all of you for your gallant help on my birthday. Be patient! I shall get stronger—I shall never give up—I shall stick to it, and this is what you too must do—stick to our task. I am trying to attune myself again with the medium, and shall improve with practice.

' I desire to confirm that it was *I* who manifested at Bletchley on the day of my birth. I was trying with all my strength to let my dear ones know that I was there. You do not understand the difficulties we have in coming through . . .' (A spasm of coughing ensued). ' All right, I shall overcome this—wait ' (a pause of some moments). Then, ' Hold it, White Eagle! hold it for me! I so want to do it! '

As we watched we saw White Eagle's presence ' grow ' on the medium. Then followed White Eagle's invocation:

' Great White Spirit of the open sky, the wide prairies and the quiet valleys; Thou who dost dwell in the mighty places of the heavens, and dost speak within the human heart as it waits on Thee in its quiet hours; O spirit of truth and love, we come. We love Thee, O Father of Love; may we deem it a gift of Thine that we are given opportunity of serving Thee by sacrifice of desire. O God, we pray for Thy power on our labours.'

White Eagle continued: ' Our brother is very disturbed, very anxious to speak with you. It means so much to him that his new realisation of truth should be made known; it means all the difference between heaven and hell. Finding these things are true he must needs give them forth. It does not matter what opponents say. God will fight for him. He is out for the universal truth, out to spread those fuller truths which he has come back to bring. If you could but see from his present point of view of how little account is any human personality! Yet, since a well-known name may be used to bring this universal truth through into the hearts of men, in so far as the man Conan Doyle is concerned, let him be that channel.

' There are still many folk who cannot reconcile the teachings of Spiritualism with the outworking of laws divine and immutable. When A.C.D. arrived on the spirit side of life he found contact with the earth was not as easy as he had once thought. A great sea of astral memories tosses between the two aspects of life, and mediums can tap these unconsciously. He found that the one vital thing had been the inner and secret thought-life of his soul. All that he had ever *thought* now became his world. Thus, after death the souls of men enter into a world which is really *self-created*, and their heaven reveals itself as that which was once within their secret heart. Bearing this fact in mind, much that has been accepted as evidence of survival and spiritual life is open to question. Real evidence can only be found in spiritual contact of heart with heart. Man has only power to see a spirit with his own quickening spirit. Evidence must be spiritually discerned or else may only consist of husks, mere figments; although there are of course exceptions to this rule. A.C.D.'s one desire is to make a re-statement which will eventually clear out of Spiritualism all that is unreal and confusing. His soul is charged, and has clearer teaching to unfold, a glorious mission to fulfil. In the light of this teaching only will the Memorial be built, for there can be no advance otherwise.

'The Conan Doyle Memorial is not in the hands of the Spiritualists (as they are to-day) but is being watched over by the universal Light. Until all are united in aim they cannot advance. Yet the noble work wrought by Arthur Conan Doyle cannot be halted but must ever progress. Now that he has deeper knowledge of the after-life and its conditions he will still lead its advance.'

White Eagle was asked if he could obtain a clearer outline of what was to come. A.C.D. then spoke. It is interesting to note the change in words and phrasing. Would that print could indicate the change in diction, manner, in the whole personality that now manifested.

A.C.D.: 'It all lies within these words—*the kingdom of heaven is within.* That is why I now see so clearly man's need for a Master. In Christ you have all; the secrets of life and death lie in his teaching. Man must take up his cross and follow the light of love, for the cross symbolises the crucifixion of all selfish aims and desires, the complete submission of the personal man to the impersonal love of God, the Creator of all. This is the secret of life both here and hereafter. Man must live not for himself, not for his good name, nor to acquire personal power or prosperity, nor for success, but to contribute to the common good. In giving all he receives all. Thus and thus only will he enter into the kingdom of heaven.

'Truly it is said that man must be born again—not of the flesh, but of the Spirit. This means that he must die to self; that every man, whether incarnate in the body or discarnate, must eventually pass through a *death of his mortal self*, and awaken into new life, into a fuller and richer consciousness of the presence of the one all-loving God. Only thus will he find himself and find again those whom he loves. From this sphere of Christ-consciousness descend all those whom you love, who have entered the spiritual life; and until you can raise yourself in spirit, attune yourself to their light, your power of communication with them must lack something most beautiful and pure.

Consider the gulf that was fixed between the Rich Man and Lazarus; the bridgeless gulf which, after all, was of man's own creation. Yet there was still one way to cross that gulf, the way of love; but not, mark you, any personal or possessive kind of love, but rather the impersonal love of self-giving, self-forgetting, and self-sacrifice.

' *Unless a man is born again he can in no wise enter the kingdom of heaven.* This is true indeed; yet there remain some souls which are still bound closely to earth, and which seek to regain contact with earthly things through the channels provided by mediumship. They too need showing the better way; for the veil between this world and yours is thin indeed compared to the severance between the earthly man, even when discarnate, and the real man of heaven.

' We make a mistake when we stress the importance of this, that or the other person, forgetting that there must always be mutual co-operation in the spreading of eternal truth. That is why I would prefer no personal reference in the Memorial Appeal (were this possible), since you are working not for a person but for a principle, for an ideal which will embody both the broad charity of the Christian teaching and the pure principles of Christ; or of the great White Light of Truth, it matters not whether interpreted through Buddha, Krishna or any other master.

' My wife will admit that I was a man of strong opinions out of which I was not easily persuaded. Nevertheless, Spiritualism eventually compelled me to admit certain facts. I changed my mind again when I accepted the leadership of Jesus Christ in the movement of Spiritualism. Again I change concerning the after-death state. Surely, surely, my friends would expect a man to have greater knowledge and clearer vision when freed from the limitations of the earthly tabernacle? Else where would progress be?

' I am not prepared to say more at the moment. These things cannot be forced. I am content to leave them in the hands of God. . . . This is the chosen instrument or channel for this special work, but another means will shortly be used to satisfy those who will require proof of a more material nature. The Wise Knight (with whom I am in close contact) has arranged for us to meet again soon. This is the kind of gathering I like best and think likely to bring the best results.

' I am to endeavour to give you *this material proof on a photographer's plate* (turning to Mrs. Caird). You are very necessary for this.

' White Eagle once called me Brother Nobleheart—I should like this name to be mine in your thoughts. Tell the brethren in Paris that I am deeply grateful for their aid, which has linked me with their Wise Knight for a mission which will prove itself as time progresses.'

It will be remembered that A.C.D. said that he was shortly preparing to give a more material proof of his identity—a proof on a photographic plate. At that time only two mediums were available in England for psychic photography (and there are still very few). Mrs. Caird managed to secure an appointment with a Mrs. Deane, at the Stead Library, on the following day, and to her delight received the picture of A.C.D. as promised. The photograph itself will be seen to be an extraordinary production, because psychic photography itself is one of the most chancy and hit-or-miss varieties of mediumship. Perhaps once in six or once in a dozen times do the features of the desired person in spirit appear on the plate. More often there comes the face of a stranger, or of someone still on earth known or unknown to the sitter. All too often the faces look as immobile and lifeless as masks or as plaster-of-paris casts. This of A.C.D. has been claimed as the best of all psychic pictures. Be this as it may, it is worth careful study for its animation, good humour and benevolence, and for the sense of life which invests it. It differs from any other psychic painting or portrait of Sir Arthur, whom Mrs. Caird herself had never met personally. Lastly, the photographic medium herself knew nothing of Mrs. Caird's association with the A.C.D. work.

So there the photograph stands, as a testimony not only to A.C.D. but to the Wise Knight behind him, for it was the latter's power which enabled it to be secured with such ease and

certainty and indeed made it possible. Mrs. Caird went many times afterwards to try to obtain a second picture of A.C.D., but in vain. It was again the Master's power which was lending life to this message from A.C.D., a power which originates from beyond astral realms and contacts, as we shall see later. By this photograph A.C.D. signed, sealed and delivered his message of the 22nd. This was one proof—but not the conclusive proof which was to come later and, as M. Bhotiva said, would 'crash all critics'; but substantial nevertheless.

CHAPTER X

'YOU CAN SEE FOR YOURSELVES—I AM A HAPPY MAN'

'People ask me what it is which makes me so perfectly certain Spiritualism is true. That I am perfectly certain is surely demonstrated by the fact that I have abandoned my congenial and lucrative work and subjected myself to all sorts of inconveniences, losses and even insults in order to get the facts home to the people.'

Sir Arthur in a Letter.

At the next meeting on June 22nd, M. Bhotiva was again present. It will be noted that the group met when possible on the 22nd of a month, this being a day of power so far as the A.C.D. work was concerned.

White Eagle spoke first: 'It may interest you to know that I was aware of this particular work before Arthur passed from the body. I already knew about it when I spoke to a group in Wales about twelve months ago (Miss Mary Conan Doyle and Minesta were on holiday there) when I gave a good deal of information which will be valuable some day. Long after your own passing, this work will go onwards. A.C.D. comes. He is so happy: now he speaks.'

A.C.D.: 'Cannot you see that by my old face in the picture? That is what *you* have produced—it is *your* power in this group which has sent to them (to his family) a message so that they will now know how I am feeling about things, and that I am a happy man. This you can see for yourselves in the picture.

'I want you to compare this impression of myself (which we were able to imprint on a photographic plate) with some of the spirit-photographs received by others. I particularly want a close comparison, for this will teach you much. I want you to realise the difference between an 'astral impression' and the real thing. For this is the very truth we are determined to make clear. There is so much humbug about these psychic things—largely unconscious, I admit—but what is needed is sane discrimination between the substantial and the nebulous type of proof. This is what Spiritualism's critics, good men at heart, stand out for. You must help your people to discriminate between the real and the unreal. This does not lessen but will rather increase their strength to mount to a spiritual consciousness which will reveal reality.

'My mission is to indicate the difference between what is foolish and nonsensical, and what is a jewel of eternal truth. The truth will reveal heaven itself; the false will make a fool of a man. So long as a man remains enmeshed in intellectual pride he can never find truth. With this I am afraid some of my friends will disagree. Yet I must insist that "*Except a man become as a little child he can in no wise enter the Kingdom of Heaven.*" I stress this again and again.'

A questioner: 'Will you define " *except a man become as a little child* "?'

A.C.D.: 'Except a man be stripped of all pride and egotism; except he realise that he is *nothing* without the power of Almighty Spirit; unless a man breaks out from the prison-house of arrogance to an understanding that *of himself he can do nothing*—he is dulled to the glories of heaven.

'Each soul must eventually be stripped of all possessions, whether of mind or heart, and stand forth naked, an infinitesimal *nothing* bathed in a vast ocean of universal knowledge and power. The man must literally go through the valley of death, not of the physical body, but of *himself*, naked of all things. . . .

'Then and then only for him can the Light dawn. For then the spiritual sunlight breaks on the way, which is also the truth and the life. Thus only can there come growth in power, peace and joy to the soul entering on the universal, to the babe-in-spirit about to grow to spiritual manhood in the tender and everlasting arms.

'Has it never seemed strange to you that the souls of men of forcefulness and intellectual power should never return from the unseen to communicate with the men of earth? The answer lies in the foregoing. They cannot.

' I look to all of you here to put forward this message of mine, which will increase in power and clarity as I become more accustomed to this medium. You realise my utter dependence on you to give this message to the world? I am sure you will be faithful.

' I can but hope that what I am able to tell you will clear away the doubts of those who question and the credulity of those who too readily accept the teachings of Spiritualism. No words of mine can detract one iota from the great love and true communion which can assuredly take place between those on earth and those in spirit. Not for one instant would I shake the belief of thousands who have received comfort from knowledge of the spirit world; I would give a higher conception of it, something not only ennobling to the Spiritualists themselves but to the whole community. We work for an impersonal, for a more divine love to be brought into the hearts of men, so that they may live in truth as brothers rather than only talk about brotherhood. I hold no other desire. May God grant it! I believe that He will give me the power and opportunity to carry this message to the uttermost parts of the earth.

' Even then I do not speak of immediate or wide success. What is required of you is to be as babes, ready to be guided, ready to be used as willing channels for the power of the spirit. This may seem an ideal, perhaps; but only in fulfilling it will you find your joy, your own kingdom of heaven. You may well thank God for the opportunity which is offered.

' God bless old White Eagle! He is one of the shining ones! To you he is just old White Eagle; *to us* something more; but sufficient be it that he is just your loving companion. Let us leave it there.'

Now follows the record of the next meeting.

White Eagle: ' In the silence, in your hearts, know God's love. Then you cannot fail. Those assembled here have placed a sacred trust on you. God sees purity of heart and sincerity of purpose, and knows that in spite of the dross and weariness of the flesh a spiritual illumination will pour through these channels. We desire you to continue, but only at intervals as the power assembles. For at present only a small amount of material can come through at any one time; but we shall endeavour to give *quality* in the message.'

A.C.D. continued after a long pause.

' When I have managed to adjust myself better to the medium we will continue our pleasant little talk. It requires a certain amount of practice, I find—that is, in the control of the physical body of the medium—to be able to give through her consecutive and clear ideas (taps meditatively with fingers of right hand on chair). Yes, yes, yes—let us just have a friendly chat. I think it is easier, so that we warm up to our subject later—yes, a friendly chat is the best way to commence.

' I used to think that everything was very easy in the spirit world. In fact, I made a point of painting pretty pictures of it. I would not take away one iota of anyone's belief and hope; but I would like now to give a clearer idea of the state to which one passes after leaving the physical body. It is extremely difficult to explain to a finite mind the actual facts concerning the mental state of the individual soul after the change of death; because a different experience comes to each man, so one cannot lay down any hard and fast rules. There is nevertheless a state, or intermediate condition through which one passes, the experience lasting perhaps for a few days, weeks, months, or continuing for many hundreds of years. . . . . . '

Question: What was your first impression after passing?

' It was entirely different from what I had expected, and that is what most people, Orthodox and Spiritualist alike, will find —a very different summerland or heaven from what they had expected. The nature of that new life turns largely on the quality of the new arrival's mentality, but still more on what his attitude has been during his former life towards his fellows and towards human life in general. That is to say, a man may find himself much better off in the next life than he or anyone else had anticipated; on the other hand he may find himself in complete bondage.

'The power to create, either mentally or physically, is the gift of every man. On his creative power rests the crux of the whole business of the after life. The man of ability whose bent lies in the creating of characters in literature, or in the painting of pictures, or the writing of poetry—in the creation either of beauty or the reverse by his *positive creative thought*—is very surely creating his environment and his habitation when he is freed from the flesh.

'What of my first impressions? Well, I can speak only for myself. Everyone does not at once realise that he has passed out of his physical body. One seems to be in process of leaving but has not actually left. One is still able to see, and to some extent contact, earth and earth conditions. It is rather a terrible sensation when one endeavours to express oneself to one's friends and is unable to make any impression on them; and when some souls here find (as they do) their former deeds are still working evil in the minds and hearts of souls on earth, it is terrible to be unable to arrest the forces one has loosed.

'That is the main idea; that the creations of one's own brain go on and on like the waves of a rolling sea that are ever beating against the minds of many fellow creatures. When these creations are beautiful, it is a heavenly and immeasurable joy to see the good in them radiating through the human universe; but when it is otherwise . . . I dare paint no picture of this state.

'I would explain that there are differing degrees of mental activity in the spiritual world. The more highly developed is the released soul mentally and spiritually, the greater will be the degree of joy it will experience; whereas in the lower grades of astral life, the light and shade effect on the soul is not so apparent.

'Astral memories and interferences: I intend to deal fully with that question because there is so much in Spiritualism of—I would not say untruth—but of misrepresentation. You have already, of course, gained some knowledge of the power of thought, and are perhaps aware that a thought in your own mind if powerful enough can be photographed. If you will compare a spirit photograph of myself (lately published in a psychic journal) with the photograph you yourselves have received, you will observe that the former lacks intelligence and vitality; while the latter gives, I flatter myself, an intelligent representation.

'This lack of intelligence and vitality can be found throughout the phenomena of Spiritualism—in manifestations by means of ouija boards or materialisation, or the direct voice. These phenomena are comparable to bubbles; prick them, and if they lack a sustaining intelligence, they fall to nothing. Investigate this for yourselves by your own observation, and you will prove the existence of a great sea of etheric impression, which lingers around or clings to particular places such as the former scenes of a soul's life on earth. Unknown to the person concerned such thought-forms, if very intense, will live on. For instance, in a house much loved by its former owner people may feel " presences " passing them on stairways, hear " whisperings " in rooms, and even an apparition may appear to scare the inhabitants. These phenomena are not due to spirits, of course, but to memories that cling to places and live on. In churches and other old buildings with accumulated power many such forms and lingerings will frequently be seen by clairvoyants and described as spirits. Not at all; they are merely the thought-vibrations of a bygone age.

'I do not wish for one moment to belittle the value of all spiritualistic phenomena. Undoubtedly there are genuine manifestations. But there still remains much which is merely shadowy. There are many spheres in which human thought can manifest and these must be considered; but it must also be remembered that unprincipled spirits can manipulate astral thought-forces to suit their own mischievous purposes.

'The crux of the whole matter depends on the quality of the mind or the purity of the aspirations of the person who would communicate with a spirit. If a human mind is attuned to a spiritual sphere of love and service a perfectly intelligent communication will be the result; but if the man's mind be only nebulous, untrained and lacking in spiritual understanding, trouble of some sort will be the outcome.'

Speaking of his personal self, A.C.D. continued: ' It is not that personal part of me that I want to continue to live in the spirit world. I want to forget the old personal self of A.C.D., for over here personalities (although sweet and dear to us all) take a subsidiary place. It is the Christ Light that we should all follow. We must endeavour to bring it to clear and perfect expression in the hearts and lives of men. When I think of my former errors of thought, and when I see what resulted from them; oh, my anguish! oh, my despair! Dear God, I ask no more than to be able to give a clearer description of this truth to others! Only one thing in human life truly matters, and this is that men should realise for themselves the redeeming power of Christ's love. For only if the Christ spirit is awake in them, is abiding within them, *do they live!* All these phenomena, all this continual running to mediums by people who want to keep in continual touch with the dead, is wrong. Men must seek rather for the living light of truth, and for realisation of the redeeming love—which knowledge of the laws governing human survival may help them to understand. Only with this object in view should men seek to lift the veil between the two worlds.'

CHAPTER XI

COMMUNICATION AND COMMUNION

'The phenomena under consideration (namely, psychic or super-normal phenomena) are incomparably the most important among all the facts presented to us by the whole of experience from the philosophical point of view, so that it is the duty of every man of science to get acquainted with them and study them thoroughly.'
—Schopenhauer.

At the next meeting A.C.D. returned to this important theme.
' SOMETIMES we see those people who can act as mediums as a light radiating through the fog which envelops the earth, and we must make contact with that light as best we can. Picture yourself in a London street on a foggy winter's night, and you will see how the earth looks to us, and perhaps grasp some of our difficulties. Yet it need not always be so. Sometimes when we return and find things clear-cut and true, the mind of the medium happy and bright with no ripple of depression or worry to disturb reception, we are able to sail in and make a clear impression on her brain. It is comparatively rare, however, to get a perfectly clear and definite message through, since there is always a residue of the medium's mentality through which we have to press. Mediumship is a fine art as well as a calling; and as mankind in general is only just awaking to the value of the spiritual life, mediums themselves remain strangely ignorant of the increased powers which might be theirs. It is necessary for a medium to be well balanced, sane, sound and true.

' The majority of the communications received by the Spiritualists come from the denizens of the higher astral, from souls both good in intention and pure in motive, although of limited knowledge and outlook. What they pass on is more or less their own personal opinion. For this reason we find that many controls in spiritualistic circles set out only their own

viewpoint and outline their own ideas. For he who dwells in
the astral spheres narrows down his experience of the after-life,
much as a man on earth clings to fixed opinions, political or
religious. Maybe he thinks that he possesses the whole truth,
and that his convictions are final. Every soul, however—and
this is important—must eventually walk that path whereon he
becomes *cleansed from all assertion*. It is of this heaven world
that I would continue to speak tonight.

' The Spiritualist may not declare that in his contact with the
first three or four or even seven astral planes he has found all
heaven. He has yet far to go and will find many snares, pitfalls,
and illusions in his contacts with the astral. Psychic or magnetic
forces which surround the human environment are often
responsible for phenomena which are too readily accepted as
evidence of communication from a spirit. Much can be found
in the sitter's own mentality and magnetism to account for these;
and then also there are deceiving spirits which find their amuse-
ment in the impersonation of well-known personalities. This
I have myself witnessed with some disquiet.

' Sometimes a medium will himself create a thought-form
which in time becomes so endowed with animation as to attach
itself to its creator, be seen by other clairvoyants, and actually
give messages through its medium. This also I have seen.

' This is not necessarily due to conscious fraud. Many people
when they come into Spiritualism strongly desire to become
mediums. Circles for development are formed, and when the
sitter is told that he has mediumistic powers a condition of
self-hypnotism can take place. A thought-form can thus become
so "backed" and clothed that it becomes realistic. We have
already said that astralities—and these are also astralities—are
merely dead things, or masks which can be easily detected. Any
true spiritual contact holds always its own ring of truth.

' It is certainly not wrong, nor is it undesirable, for you to
seek communion with those in the spirit life. Neither is it
wrong for you to give your friends an opportunity of returning
to communicate. In many instances such communication is of
the utmost value and help to both of the parties concerned. But

having had that experience, the man in the spirit world having been able to send his messages of reassurance, both of those concerned should realise that there is work to be accomplished in the next world which cannot be done if the spirit is continually being held back by those who mourn its passing.'

After a pause A.C.D. continued:

' It may help you to understand me better if I give my own experience of control. I find the easier way to use this particular medium is not through her subconscious but through her super-conscious mind. We have already said that man—broadly speaking—can make contact with several planes of the next life. If he be attuned only to the lower astral he must not expect anything very uplifting; but if a medium can be induced to raise his or her consciousness, so as to open up the superconscious, a true spiritual contact can be established.

' My best work through Minesta has always been through her superconscious self and not by control through the brain. Although I cannot hold her by an automatic or hypnotic control, I can pour facts and teaching through her spiritual intelligence. Therefore do not attempt to discuss these messages with her afterwards, or confuse her conscious mind with ideas. Leave her alone as much as possible, and mentally isolated. Then I can do my work.

' During that work, seen clairvoyantly, you would witness an illumination around the head which projects for two or three yards, of which the upper part tapers into a golden beam of light.

' In many communications through mediumship you will get the automatic control of which I speak. Then you will some-times see much that will remind you of departed friends, or hear short sentences so like in style and manner that the identity seems certain. It cannot be sustained for very long, however, for this is the product of the automatic trance control, which is a kind of hypnosis of mind and body. In such cases little more than an automaton will be functioning and the flow of inspiration is checked.

' Control of the superconscious self of the medium, on the

other hand, will bring about a clear and satisfactory reflection of the *nature* and *personality* rather than the mannerisms of the communicating spirit.

'There is but a small percentage of what is called "subconscious mind stuff" coming through spiritualistic channels. What is usually called "subconscious" can be attributed rather to the conscious mind of the medium interfering with the spirit control. The core or inner life of the subliminal self remains always in contact with the universal life, and thus can be and is inspired and influenced by higher beings, which usually operate in a band rather than singly.

'In our particular instance the messages are transmitted down through the spheres. Sometimes we obtain a clear channel, and are able to express our theme clearly and well, while at others there is a certain crossing of currents and vibrations, so that when we read the message afterwards, through your minds, we feel a sense of dissatisfaction and sadness. Obviously our thoughts have not reached you with the clarity we could have wished. Sometimes we find it impossible to convey our exact meaning. In spite of all these barriers the veil thins between the two worlds; and we shall find proofs of survival in the years to come will not so much depend on communications coming through recognised mediums, but rather will win acceptance because the majority of men and women will have become awakened and *alive* to the reality and presence of unseen powers around them. At present man is dulled to them, or even dead, as was Lazarus in his tomb until called to life by the Master.

'A medium's mind must be flexible and easily influenced, yet under perfect control. It is no easy matter to attain and retain this combination of self-control with the sensitivity of the visionary and idealist. Yet all this is essential before a perfectly attuned instrument can open to receive the perfect message.

'I impress on you that only in certain conditions can a shaft of pure light come through. Unquestionably, mediumship is something that can be developed and improved; but I would not advocate this development for everyone, but only for the chosen vessels. The mistake made in the Spiritualist movement is to advocate development of mediumistic faculties wholesale. As in the days of old, so today; there are souls who are chosen and dedicated to the task; for the rest the dangers of forcing psychic development cannot be over-stressed.

'Some people think that a medium becomes like an empty vessel when in a state of trance. This is not so; for although the medium's body serves to express the message of the communicating spirit, a residue of its owner's personality and mentality is retained which has to be cleared, or else penetrated. In the process of this clearing the message can become coloured more or less. This is why a medium can become either the greatest help or hindrance to a communicator.

'If a medium strives to cultivate his—or her—mentality and spirituality, that medium can become of infinite use and importance. An ignorant medium does not always make the best instrument. Should an unlettered or ignorant medium be chosen for a specific task, this choice will be due to some spiritual quality or faculty inherent in the medium. Let me impress on you that the medium's intelligence must never be overbearing, but rather so docile that it lends itself to the communicator. An ignorant medium, while useful in so far as the mind does not hold back the thoughts coming through, labours under the disadvantage of being unable to bring forth the message with clarity and force.

'We ourselves are dealing with *thoughts* which have to be expressed *in words* to make them intelligible to you. We must always clothe them with the language we find in the mentality or power of comprehension of the medium. Therefore you will see the necessity of that mind being well trained. We are hoping to use this medium in this way—perhaps Minesta will forgive an old man for saying that it is sometimes no easy matter to play a fine tune on an instrument which sometimes seems to have only one string, and that she can help much in days to come.

'Later I shall finish many a theme commenced in our earlier sittings. In this you will recognise the handiwork of an individual and outside communicator, so do not judge until you see the finished article. Before my passing I had little understanding of the many difficulties holding up communication with the spirit world, but I became convinced of the reality of that communication on cold evidence—which I now recognise might not have been so valid as I once thought. Another problem, I find, is that when I come back hundreds of ideas attempt to pour through. I must learn to regulate this overcrowding. From where I am now living I find that it is difficult to get a human mind to receive ideas from me with clarity, although this resistance is eventually overcome. I so want to link you all together in a bond which gets ever closer, for there is so much for you all to learn.'

M. Bhotiva was present at the next meeting, and Lady Conan Doyle and her family arranged to ' tune in ' from their home in Sussex.

A.C.D. (to Bhotiva): ' You have been asking for further proof, my friend, that this is Conan Doyle communicating; that it is he who has come back to bring to his friends the glad truth of life after death. I can assure you these proofs will be given. They are in the words I speak, in the talks I have already given. Even so, far more tangible proofs are yet to come, *after* the message has been delivered in its entirety.

' People will accept my message—indeed they must accept it, for so much depends on their acceptance. I am only the spokes-man for greater ones than I, and when my mission is finished I shall leave this earth and advance. I have not hurried my own family in this matter because I know they will find it difficult to accept the changed man that I am. I find that I have a certain difficulty in tuning in to the extra vibrations which are here tonight.'

A lengthy pause ensued.

A.C.D.: ' It is not finished. But I have been brought back by the thoughts of my family, who are in my old home and thinking about me. What a strong personal link I feel here tonight—quite different, quite different. You will remember that I have told you that we function on all the different planes of being, and that even from the earth man can touch all planes of being? So also with me: when I come back to earth conditions I have to attune myself to the degree of mental life possessed by those whom I contact. Thus, sometimes I speak from the astral plane, sometimes from planes above; but I have always to attune my vibration to the conditions provided.

'We must resume our discussion of these matters next week. I am now directed to speak about the work which lies ahead of us. You have been prepared for years for this work, much as I myself was prepared, although I did not realise my mission. I am under the direction of the Wise Ones. I am their servant, their instrument, and I have to organise this group, this work in London. This teaching, these messages are to be the foundation of that work. I now come back to reveal a finer life, a nobler path than had ever dawned on my earthly conception. All must be put right. Man must be taught the truth concerning his life after death. I shall give it to you. Send it out into the world. No man who really knows me, knows my thoughts and writings will ever doubt these words, they will recognise me therein; they will and must understand what I am trying to tell them.

'Why was I once inundated with prophecies of the disasters and catastrophes to which humanity is now heading? Because, as I see now, I was a pivot, a central point. Thousands then hung on my words. Because of this fact I was destined to be used by the White Brotherhood in order to bring a clearer, a truer, a more exact teaching about the life beyond death.

'In this connection you may wonder why the Conan Doyle Memorial has been kept in abeyance? The reason is that had it gone ahead it might have got into the wrong hands, been run on the wrong lines. Men's minds have to be prepared gradually for new ideas. . . .'

White Eagle said afterwards: 'Evidence is not always what the mind of man considers evidence. The unseen Brotherhood has its own way of producing evidence, and the inner self of man must be ready to receive it. Otherwise it will mean nothing to him. We say that the foundation of the English group of the Brotherhood will lie in this message, and that when this message goes out many people will accept and believe.

People will say, " This is true. We are prepared to follow."
Eventually all classes of men will be brought to believe. Your
faith and loyalty must carry this thing through. Then you will
never fail—never fail.'

CHAPTER XII

A RESUMÉ

' I have a key in my bosom called Promise; that will, I am persuaded, open any lock in Doubting Castle.'
—John Bunyan.

WHILE the Spiritualists, being familiar with the terms employed and knowing their meaning, may find these earlier A.C.D. messages comprehensible, some of those who are not Spiritualists may feel at a loss. Perhaps what follows may help, before we go on to the main A.C.D. message in Part II.

The writer once lived in an old house—all oak beams and draughts—which had been built on a site where long ago had stood a monks' hostel. Queer things used to happen. Voices, whisperings and mutterings were heard in empty rooms, and footsteps passed one on the stairs or walked across the room overhead, to and fro, to and fro, sometimes for hours. In the charming gardens was a lake with a path round it on which were frequently seen the spirit forms of three monks always together, whom we named Brothers Clement, Joseph and Amyas. In course of time we got to know the real nature or cause of the sounds, footsteps and whisperings—they were astralities, and caused by thoughts powerful enough to have impressed themselves on the etheric fabric of the building (everything having its etheric replica), where they had remained perhaps for centuries. They were not real sounds in the physical sense, although they might have been semi-physical. They were real only to those who could hear them. Sensitive folk registered these things and were sometimes frightened. Denser people, hearing and seeing nothing said it was all nonsense and were duly satisfied. One cannot be too dogmatic about the monks, for they seemed alive, interested and aware of the human folk around, unlike the cold astralities indoors. They may even have been the souls of former monks occasionally drawn back by their love for the gardens, the lake, and their associations with it. Or it may be that their thoughts and affections still linked them to their former home, animating what would have otherwise been only astralities.

What we have all to understand is that we leave traces of ourselves on the etheric world, wherever we go. Our auras impinge both on things and on people. Our auras being infused with ourselves—that is, with our personality, character and thoughts—affect everything they touch. Much depends on whether we are strong characters or not. If the former, we leave a deeper impression on the etheric world, on the substance, or etheric ' matter ' which permeates the physical. Unlike physical impressions, those on etheric matter do not fade away.

Now for another illustration, this time more fanciful; we have all heard of old houses where some famous person once slept. Elizabeth the First, for example, seems to have conferred fame on innumerable bedrooms by sleeping in them. Suppose that someone known to us happens to spend a night in one of these notable bedrooms, being unaware of its fame. Surely that person might dream about or have contact with the Queen? And if sensitive or mediumistic our friend might even receive messages from Elizabeth by, say, automatic writing, and go away elated by the honour and distinction. The message would be inanimate, of course, poor stuff, just as shades, thought-forces or astralities are inanimate. These things happen. They *exist*, they cannot be denied. Every ancient battlefield, or place of some former crime or tragedy carries the ' feeling ' of its stain of crime or sadness for centuries to come, so that sensitive people register and shrink from it. In such a world as this, with these strange happenings about us, Spiritualism has grown.

Now for another example: many Spiritualist services are held, we may say, in some public building, or in an ex-Baptist chapel or mission-hall. For owing to lack of means very few Spiritualist Churches acquire their own premises. The hall will probably bear signs of having been hastily cleared after a whist drive or dance held on the previous evening. No atmosphere of religion has been built up, and cannot be in a building which houses such diverse activities. This condition is typical of the average Spiritualist meeting. Contrary to expectation, the people attending seem normal middle class folk. As they settle down in their seats they bring an air of expectation, even of excitement. This is because the medium or exponent tonight is no other than Mrs. X, famed in the movement for her gifts. While they wait members of the audience are either reading psychic journals they have purchased at the door, or whispering among themselves. At length the chairman introduces Mrs. X, a person who looks kind, sincere and in no way remarkable or weird. After a prayer and a hymn sung with hearty emphasis rather than any display of musical talent, comes what all have been waiting for.

Mrs. X is to give a ' demonstration of psychometry '—that is, of reading the ' aura ' of articles sent up by members of the audience. Those articles are even now being collected on a tray, and presently they go up to a table beside Mrs. X. All these articles have been worn by their owners, and consist of oddments of jewellery, pens, pencils, keys, pocket-books, watches, necklaces and rings in great variety. Mrs. X bends over the tray. Everyone holds their breath. Mrs. X selects an article, and handling it continually (as though drawing forth her knowledge *out* of that article) begins her ' reading.'

She is astonishingly accurate. The first article is one which might be worn either by a man or a woman. Mrs. X makes no mistake. A description of the owner is given, of the owner's character, and of his state of health and happiness. The owner's christian name and the christian names of some of his relatives and friends who have passed on—all these are ' given out,' but none come easily. There is a feeling that a great effort of concentration goes into each ' reading '—no mere knitting of the brows or head-concentration, but concentration of the woman's whole being, of all her vital forces. ' Readings ' follow in rapid succession, nearly all being accepted, and some, giving notably detailed and accurate facts recognised with some excitement. Now the meeting is drawing to a close. Mrs. X looks played out. Another hymn is sung, and a brief prayer of benediction follows. Afterwards the audience foregather, animatedly talking things over. The weary Mrs. X is hemmed in by people who want just another private little message for themselves, and is at length rescued by the chairman.

Anyone attending that meeting for the first time would be puzzled by Mrs. X's accuracy, which was far beyond the utmost range of chance or coincidence; more puzzled still because she so often seemed to bring out happenings which had long been forgotten by the person receiving the reading, happenings which had to be recalled from deep recesses of memory; puzzled again because the audience so readily believed that everything was done by spirit people working through Mrs. X, who had only just to 'put across' their messages to someone in the audience. Could it be that everything was as simple as that? If so, why did Mrs. X get so exhausted? Far from being powerfully helped, it looked as if she was contending with great difficulties.

A stranger might not have been so puzzled had Mrs. X been out of form, or if some lesser demonstrator had only got half or a quarter of the 'readings' recognised. But this was a wonderful demonstration which did not seem in the least like mind-reading; and thought-transference was far too facile an explanation to be entertained.

An enquirer, let it be assumed, would be sufficiently interested to pay a second visit on the following week. By good fortune Mrs. X is again the demonstrator, this time of 'public clairvoyance' instead of 'psychometry.' No articles are required. The demonstrator stands on the platform and speaks direct to persons she selects among the audience, this time mostly describing 'spirit people' who, she claims, are 'with' the persons whom she addresses. Again she is very accurate, most of her descriptions being readily recognised; and one or two refused at first are later accepted by persons who at last recall the identity of the spirit while on earth. Again there seems no likelihood of thought-transference being the explanation, because recognition of some of the spirits had to be laboriously extracted from the person concerned. This is a demonstration of the extraordinary frailty or fallibility of the human memory, if of nothing else; and the whole performance is at least as puzzling as was that of the previous week. For the convinced Spiritualist the explanation which had sufficed last week sufficed again. The spirits were doing everything. Mrs. X had only to stand there and be 'used' by them. Noting the effort put forward by Mrs. X it is not easy to accept so facile an explanation. But certainly both meetings had been a wonderful demonstration of something. But of what?

They were not comparable, for instance, with the displays of 'thought' or 'mind' reading seen on public platforms or on television. They were not so slick, for one thing. 'Mind' reading or 'telepathy,' where not due to some pre-arranged system, differs widely in that it deals only with things which are *foremost* in people's minds; as when a blindfolded lady on the stage describes with complete accuracy articles held by her assistant which he has just taken from a member of the audience. With Mrs. X, however, it was often the things 'hindmost' in people's minds. She would describe happenings, or people who had died long ago, rather than more recent migrants to spirit life. This again requires consideration.

It is worth taking all possible pains to solve this problem. It has been argued in these pages that if Spiritualism is true and can truly demonstrate that men survive death, then no event of comparable importance has happened for at least two thousand years. These two demonstrations by Mrs. X, we have to realise, are typical of what is happening all over the country in Spiritualist churches and halls, where demonstrations of 'public clairvoyance' are the means most frequently employed to carry conviction to the general public. Not every demonstrator is up to the standard of Mrs. X—far from it. Otherwise our description has tried to be typical of all the others. This sort of demonstration has convinced the Spiritualists. Has it convinced our enquirer? Yes—that this had been a display of a human faculty previously unknown to him. Does it prove human survival? No. Many people feel there must be some alternative explanation. They cannot believe that the souls of men and women who have passed onward to something far more beautiful than our world can return, however much they may desire it, to conditions as crude as those which prevailed at the two meetings. This is no fault of Mrs. X's, who did her part valiantly. But intuitively some people will feel that for a real spiritual manifestation there should be beauty and harmony in the hall, and devotion on the part of the worshippers. These were mostly lacking. Where then shall we seek an explanation of these phenomena?

Here the A.C.D. message can help. He speaks of 'astral' memories. Where are they, what are they? They often remain embedded in the aura, the human aura being an extension of man's etheric body, a body which permeates his physical body. It is the etheric body which has the true sense of 'feeling.' Drive it out by a blow on the head or by an anaesthetic, and the physical body feels nothing!

The aura is an emanation extending beyond the physical body for some inches. Being a semi-material complement to the physical body it must register and retain a memory of all that has happened to that body—a memory of the people it has met and loved or hated, of the happenings which have pleased or saddened it—all these are stamped on the etheric body and aura. Thus each man bears around with him a complete record of all that has happened to himself.

Now, this aura by its nature permeates physical matter, impregnating it with itself. Therefore an article worn by anyone becomes saturated by the wearer's aura, and can be sensed or 'read' by a sensitive such as Mrs. X. Here we have the explanation for the evening of 'psychometry,' when the aura of Mrs. X read or extracted information from the aura of the article handled. She was enabled to link up instantaneously with the aura of its owner, and thereby extract additional information. This was done by an immense effort of concentration on the part of Mrs. X.

So also with the demonstration of 'public clairvoyance.' Here Mrs. X, again by a mighty effort of concentration, was so able to extend her own aura (for auras are capable of such an extension) that she could reach and draw out from the person selected the information required; Mrs. X wholeheartedly believing, as did others present, that all was being done by ' the spirits.'

Are the Spiritualists all wrong, and are we completely right in our supposition? Let us not be too sure. It is said that you can fool all the people for some of the time and some of the people all the time, but not all the people all the time. Why do the Spiritualists so wholeheartedly believe in their spirit land and people? Because they have sound reasons which were not, however, very apparent in the two meetings described.

One cannot lay down hard and fast rules about these subtle matters, or declare that these Spiritualistic phenomena consist of mere auric readings or ' husks,' with never a real spiritual contact. It is possible, even likely; the more material the people and their outlook, the less reverent the service and the conditions of the building which houses it, the more probably will our explanations fit. For these are the sort of things which can be ' pricked like bubbles ' and fall away.

Still our explanation is insufficient. Something remains. The something which not only remains but prevails is human love. If there be pure, selfless love, strong and vibrant in the heart of any one of those present in the audience, the power of that love might reach out and call a loving presence or message back from the spirit realms. Such a contact is possible. Then, instead of a dreary recital of astralities or *auralities* (to coin a word), something real, poignant and sometimes intensely moving happens, such as the startling overshadowing of the medium by the actual spirit who is trying to communicate, so that his identity is proved beyond all shadow of doubt, not by anything he says but by the manifestation of his inmost spirit, his personality, mannerisms and characteristics through the medium. This, then, is the strength of Spiritualism.

PART II

THE MESSAGE

OF

ARTHUR CONAN DOYLE

FOREWORD TO PART II

'Ignorance is the curse of God, knowledge the wing where-
with we fly to Heaven.'

'For of the soule the body forme doth take,
For soule is forme, and doth the body make.'
—Spenser, *The Faerie Queene*

LITTLE has yet been said which can give any real idea of the
conditions ruling when A.C.D. spoke at the later series of meetings when he gave the full import of his message. That which
follows is an eye-witness account taken, slightly abbreviated,
from *Thy Kingdom Come*. It first describes the little upper room
furnished as a chapel in which the meetings were held, the great
power which gathered there, and the spiritual upliftment of all
present as White Eagle opened the meetings with prayers of
deep sincerity which filled the listeners with the wonder and
awe of God.

'It was strange to see the day-to-day personality of Minesta
sink into abeyance when White Eagle came. After the prayer
followed a change. White Eagle had gone and the medium
became absolutely still. The presence of another personality
gradually became evident. For I saw the medium's form settle
in the chair, the hands fall loosely, as in the characteristic attitude
of someone else. Occasionally a hand would lift to stroke and
meditatively smooth an upper lip, as if a heavy moustache hung
there. Then again the figure settled. The face was now changed,
almost remoulded, so far as a person's face is capable of change.
The face now actually became, it was witnessed, like the face of
A.C.D. The voice now held a northern burr, whereas Minesta's
voice is clear, her words clipped. Now the voice sometimes
slurred its words.

'Slowly fell the words at first, each sentence building up upon
another. The glow of the lamp fell on the wall beyond, lighting

an engraving of the Master which hung there. Wonderful indeed
was the sense of the power of the spirit within those walls. The
voice continued, now swept along as by a torrent, now silenced
as if by the glory of some vision that it was about to try to form
into words; now, stroke by stroke, like a smith at an anvil,
beating out thought into expression in words. Then after a
period came a check, heralding always a change of subject;
a pause while the mind behind switched over to a new theme.
Then again came the steady torrent of words. Or perhaps there
would come a mistake, the beginning of a sentence to which
the mind behind could not see a logical ending. Then came a
crisp " Stop—score that out! " The voice would then retrace
and recommence the particular message.

' Yet all this time, one side of my mind was noting how
strangely formal, even businesslike the gathering was. Apart
from a few words of greeting, it was obvious that the speaker
was continuing a theme from where it had ended a week or more
ago, and that every atom of power, every moment of time must
be utilised to the full. So also, when the meeting drew to a close
and all the power was spent, the speaker would conclude with
just a word of thanks, a message of affection or a blessing, and
a brief farewell.

' I shall long remember—indeed, I shall never forget—the
passionate earnestness of the speaker, his purposeful voice, his
forceful gesture as he attempted to emphasise some meaning not
wholly clear in words. This was in truth a wonderful experience.'

The period of reception for these final messages was about
seven months, ending on June 1st, 1932; which was almost two
years since the first contact had been made with A.C.D. after
his passing. The account which we have just quoted will, it is
hoped, serve to set the scene for the reader; so that from now on—
throughout this Second Part of the book—the messages can be
given without further comment or interruption. For the con-
venience of the reader, the brief words of greeting and farewell
with which A.C.D. began and ended his discourses have been

omitted, and the discourses themselves arranged in ordered sequence. Only some of the prayers with which White Eagle opened the meetings, before A.C.D. took over the control, have been placed at the head of the chapters, but, to distinguish them, in italic type. Apart from these all that follows in this Part proceeds from A.C.D. himself; it is he alone who now speaks.

CHAPTER I

MAN'S REALISATION OF HIMSELF,
AND OF A LIFE EVER MORE ABUNDANT

'Fearlessness, singleness of soul, the will always to strive for wisdom . . . be the signs of him whose feet are set on that fair path which leads to heavenly birth.'
—Krishna.

' We call upon the centres of Love, Wisdom and Power, and we worship at the foot of the Cross, the Emblem of Sacrifice and renunciation of all personal aims and desires. We seek to be at-one with Thee, Divine and Living Christ, the Great White Light. We await Thy coming, O Spirit of Love. We worship Thee, and through Thy Love may the truth of life beyond death of the body dawn upon man, so that all fear of death be lifted from man, woman, and child. May they have clear vision of the progress and beauty which opens before them. Thus shall man come to know his brother and to love him, even as Thou hast loved ALL. *So mote it be!'*

I

I FIND myself in an unspeakably beautiful 'heaven world'. I desire above all things to be able to bring such a reality as this home to my friends; but I also realise only too well that it can be shared only if they can understand the nature of the heaven to which I have gone. All this has made me feel a deeper urge to spread the truth concerning the after-life. I believe that during my earth-life I have already won something of a reputation as a missionary. I carry on this work still for the people of earth, but by different ways and means from those which I used to follow. How difficult it is to make a true contact with the earth and its people! All is so different from what I once anticipated. A true conception of the real life of the spirit has yet to dawn upon man. Thank God, the mists begin to thin, so that I can see with a clearer vision than once seemed possible. Can it be that my friends still expect me to talk with them about the trivialities of the personal earth life? I have now done with trivialities, having found the realities of man's being and existence. Yet, shall I ever find it possible to paint, with the language which I find at my disposal in the mind of Minesta, any adequate picture of the glory, wonder and beauty of heaven? Yes, it can, it must be attempted; it must be done.

It is a fact that after passing through what are known as the astral places we shed a ' shell '—the ' dress ' or ' envelope ' which once contained or housed the soul during its astral life. This ' shell ' or body remains in that astral condition from which we ' die ' to rise again to true spiritual life, and it can be reanimated or resurrected temporarily by psychic powers. Note, this is purely an artificial animation, but can appear to a medium as a reality, as a real spirit person. This is why we wish to raise people's minds to a truer appreciation of the life of the spirit, for in this alone can they make real contact with those who have passed on. Let us remember, however, that a large percentage of people living in the astral worlds have no desire whatever to return to earth, being no longer interested either in its progress or the people they have left behind. That is why it is not for everyone to seek out or try to force communication between the so-called dead and the living.

I repeat that in this new life of mine intercourse between the two worlds proves not nearly so simple as I had been led to think; nevertheless, *communion*, holy communion, between soul and soul can be a more glorious reality than is yet understood. Indeed, psychic communications as they are accepted today must some day give place to this truer communion of spirit between incarnate and arisen souls. At present the *personal* aspect of communication is over-stressed; personal memories are mostly sought after, and if forthcoming are regarded as evidence of

identity and proof of an after-life. Yet while these personal
traits and mannerisms can endear a soul to its former friends on
earth it is well to remember that these may prove to be a pitfall,
indicating that there exists too much surface relationship and
insufficient recognition or understanding of the needs of man's
spirit.

Here, then, lies a basis from which much of the Spiritualism of
the future will evolve. It must change from that present free-
and-easy, happy-go-lucky contact of the man of earth with the
personal selves of those people who have passed on, thereby
stimulating personal memories of earthly pleasures, desires and
happenings; and grow into a deeper understanding between
souls, and through that a deeper recognition of the spiritual needs
of each soul. When such a *reality of reunion* becomes a part and
parcel of the soul-life of the man still incarnate and of the man
discarnate, then mortal man's fear of transient things such as
sickness, poverty and death will be swept away. For this same
spirit which will quicken in man is the very Spirit of the living
Christ, and can heal the ills of all people. ' *For He shall wipe
away all tears. . . .* '

With all the strength of my newly-released spirit I desire to
reveal to my new friends that new man which is Doyle. I am
no longer concerned with the many trivialities of the old earth-
life, or of earthly affairs, except in so far as these affect the
spiritual development of the person concerned—not, alas, that I
can greatly help the individual save by telling him about the
foundation of the spiritual life. Yes, yes; the old Doyle seems
to be passing, but I will prove to you all that while I die yet I
live again! Yes. *But there are no trimmings left on a man when
he has passed the Second Death.* Only his purified spirit remains
after that supreme experience . . . Oh, that second awakening!
Then was I conscious of only one thing; of only one thing!—
and that was the wonder, the infinitude, the allness of God's
love for me and for all men.

In that supreme moment I knew that there could be no such
thing as separate existence apart from God. For at that moment
the personality which separates man from God had died, while

his individuality had been reborn. For then I saw before me a great pulsating throng of spiritual life and being, into which had passed all the souls of men who had lived in innocence and forgetfulness of self. As units of this mighty host of souls, those who have passed through an earth life—*which is really an earth-death*—quicken and *live*, giving forth from themselves with gladness and with joy all that will benefit God's mighty Plan for men.

NOT for a moment do I wish to destroy the beliefs of Spiritualism. Not so; rather am I trying to bring back a larger, wiser and finer understanding of this glorious truth of survival and of communion with the beyond.

But not with everyone there; some men pass onwards weary in mind and spirit to a condition of dreaminess wherein they live for long periods, just breathing, as it were. Other souls speedily traverse the lower spheres, shed the dense astral body which is theirs on quitting the still denser physical body, and enter the heaven world. Realise that only in a state of consciousness such as this is the soul of man brought face to face with his Judgment, or with God. When faced with this Judgment—*which is but a man's realisation of himself as he truly is*—he is able to look back once and for all into his own depths. Aware at last of his own frailty when set beside the radiance and glory of the Godlike life, he is filled with compassion towards all men, and with that redeeming love of Christ which can also redeem his own soul. New ways open for him. He can go forward, onward, upward, leaving the earth plane behind for ever, onward and upward into ever higher and more wondrous realms of spiritual consciousness and understanding, ever opening himself to the inflow of a life ever more abundant; or he can be arrested by a bitter cry, by the anguish of those sorely struggling in shadow and sorrow on the earth. Is it for that soul to ignore this heart cry of humanity? Who shall say?

'*Rest in peace.*' Yes, at last I understand those words. For had you ever experienced the peace, the tranquillity and the restful beauty of the heaven world you would realise that there are many who would choose to rest in peace in such conditions. Does not man on earth also seek rest after strenuous labours?

I find that I do not like the personal pronoun very much now. It has become 'we' instead of 'I'. And this is how every man will feel after his entry into that realm of spiritual life where there is no separation either from his fellows or from God. Although the *individuality* of a man can become greater here than you on earth can well conceive, in its greatness it becomes unified with the whole, with all creation, with all living creatures. Thereafter no person speaks of himself as 'I', because he thinks in terms of 'we' in place of 'I'. Man will then know that he can neither think, speak nor act entirely of himself, because his every thought, word and act has an effect on the entire community.

We—*we!* Did not the Master Jesus say, 'Of myself I can do nothing'? Does not the truly great man say, 'I am nothing'? Feeling himself nothing he becomes a sharer with God in everything; he becomes all—an infinite being in an infinite universe. Does this seem like undue humility? No. This is one of the first and most necessary lessons a man learns when he has passed the Second Death.

Spiritualism has a vital message to bring, because some souls newly released from physical life need contact with those left behind when they first come over here. Then communication between the two states of life is right and true. The fault arises when there is clinging by earthly people to an arisen soul which should pass onward. To establish true communion man must always seek for a pure spiritual contact, which is never obtainable through the cruder forms of psychic phenomena.

II

OH, the ineffable longing which is in my heart to bring back the great truth of the heaven world of the discarnate to men! It seems an age since I left my body.

Today, I believe, is my birthday on earth;* and although most people would consider this long passed and finished so far as I am concerned, yet the links of the earth seem to hold. The day of a spirit's incarnation in the flesh is always a day of power for that spirit, and can be used for either good or evil. Thus on the anniversary of a birth, a death, or of any happening which vitally affects a human soul, the psychic vibrations will recur at the scene of that experience.

I seem now to be far removed from earth memories—that is, to a point. Experiences which were trivial have faded, and only those which deeply affected me remain. The memory of much that I wrote has also vanished, while other works of my pen and imagination I know will live on—live on, sometimes to sadden, at others to inspire. Thank God that many a writing of mine dwells in my heart as a glowing memory of happiness.

As I am speaking—or shall we rather say, pouring my spirit through this human channel which was so long prepared for this special task—I am caught up again in a ray of power and can express with increased vigour my experiences since my release.

In very truth a man does not fall into a honeypot when he passes from the earth to the spirit world. Of course, everything depends on his mental and spiritual quality at the time of his release. He who has lived a life which was grossly material, sensual and selfish will find himself in 'queer street'. Understand, my friends, that the human soul must pass once again through every condition or phase of desire which it has formerly encouraged— pass through while still remaining the conscious self which had grown so familiar—longing, yearning, desiring with all its being to gratify the thirst and hunger for similar experiences which now torture its astral body, and unable in most cases even to obtain alleviation. In course of time the man is shattered, as it were driven by unquenched longings, until at last the realisation dawns that the grey astral plane is barren of anything likely to gratify him. No picture can really paint, no description do

---

* This section—a more detailed account of the astral planes—was given later on May 22nd, 1932; that is to say, on A.C.D.'s second earthly birthday after his passing into the Beyond.

more than attempt to speak of a man's life while driven by these longings through this underworld of the coarser astral plane. Of course, eventually and inevitably the man reaches a state of exhaustion because the fire of his being has all but flamed away. As a last resort his soul cries upon God. Where else can it turn in its last extremity? As soon as this aspiration to God finds birth, when at last the soul cries, ' My God, why hast Thou forsaken me?'—then, according to the man's capacity, some tiny germ of the divine quickens, sufficient in itself to awaken a desire for more. Still the soul passes onwards, traversing the underworlds. Its every step to salvation must be earned. Even in the next sphere, the grey astral, which is lighter and brighter, the same law of salvation by effort operates. Not even there will the soul obtain satisfaction, but must strive ever onward and upward.

My friends, there is always the other side of the picture. While a man may suffer tortures of mind and body both on earth and afterward in the world beyond, there are always times when he can and does attain the heights. So far as the earth life is concerned we have always to remember that we come back into incarnation by our own volition. By right of the power of choice inherent in us, we volunteer for, we accept earthly conditions such as the ego, the true inner man, knows will yield the most valuable experiences during an incarnation. Do not imagine that any man's time of birth, or place of birth, or condition or environment of birth, happens by accident. The whole of his earth life, which is meant as a focal point from which a succeeding life in the beyond will evolve, must eventually fall into accord with a definite and divine Plan. With what precise knowledge of this plan did the Master Jesus speak when he said: '. . . *a sparrow shall not fall on the ground without your Father. But the very hairs of your head are all numbered.*'

Such is very truth. The whole Plan lies in the Mind of God; and He holds you ever in the cup of His Hand.

What man has to learn is to support himself through all experiences by means of his own courage and effort. He must not only find his real self, but also gain control over his own nature. Until this happens he cannot begin to realise the tremendous potentialities of his spirit.

The object of all life's discipline and experience is to awaken man to such a realisation. By the word 'life' I mean the soul's existence, not as you see it through mortal eyes but as a *whole*; as one vast experience passing from its apex, which is God; and travelling the full cycle of its existence, to return to that apex once more.

Yes, yes; I can speak of these things because I was given a glimpse of these heaven worlds. Sometimes I seem to be lifted up, to be borne as on angels' wings, to see these surpassing wonders revealed.

Perhaps I have spoken too gravely about the underworlds. Do not mistake me; I have said before that in many cases—in most cases—these underworld conditions are never experienced. The newly released soul can rapidly traverse them while in an unconscious state. Then they make but a dim impression, much as when you dream at night. To such souls, which have set their hearts higher, they remain only like a dream (thank God); and most of them will wake on the plane known to the Spiritualist as the 'Summerland', and there find a comfort and peace. On this subject you may have many questions to ask. I will try to give lucid answers.

Question: *I assume from your teaching that the seventh astral plane is the underworld of desires and lusts ?*

Yes, the lowest astral plane is one of burning and persistent desire, all of which the sufferer has engendered and fostered during his earth life. Those who go there are souls which have lived with neither consideration nor affection for any creature but themselves.

You will ask about the plane above? Well, there we find life a little brighter. Although it is still shadowed with a greyness like that of a November morning, a dim light shines here and there, because the inhabitants are developing affection for something, although perhaps only for nature or for animals. Throughout the soul's journey through the spheres, light comes only because the inner self is awakening. Stunted trees and vegetation become visible but the inhabitants still dwell in mists and are themselves clothed in grey. Being in fact wrapped up in self-centredness they still create for themselves similar clothing and environment. In this manner does their self-centredness become outwardly actualised in a perfectly logical and natural manner.

Question: *What about the next, the third astral plane?*

Here we find brighter conditions, because there is a desire to do something for the fellow-next-door, a wakening interest in one's neighbour. Here normal earth conditions tend to reproduce themselves. We gather for public worship, we dwell in houses which are perhaps somewhat dilapidated and not over salubrious. Again, *the inward spiritual conditions* of the inhabitants become externalised in this manner. Men's souls here, however, are striving towards the light, and this is why conditions grow more hopeful, more harmonious.

We pass to the fourth plane, where things are decidedly better. Now we find beautiful scenery, happier and on the whole finer conditions than on earth. We see the types of home described in many Spiritualist books, the lakes, rivers, mountains, flowers and animals. This is in all a bright second edition or continuation of a comfortable life lived on earth. Here the soul has attained to some mental and spiritual development, and having thus attained begins to create these conditions of harmony and beauty *out of itself*; for they are after all only the reflex of the soul's mental and spiritual level. Cannot you understand the reason why this should be? Paradoxical though it will appear, these conditions come about because the human spirit is at last able to modify the conditions and environment which surround it *from itself—from out of itself*; much as a man on earth is continually contributing harmony (or disharmony) to his family and home life. This is why, and how, comfort, serenity, harmony and beauty come into being in the next life.

Question: *If the astral planes number seven, how can this be reconciled with the dominant number, twelve? You have given us seven astral, three mental and three celestial planes, thirteen in all?*

There are actually twelve planes. The seventh or lowest

astral is so closely interwoven with the earth, so identified with earthly interests and influence that it should be considered with the earth. The first real astral is the first grey plane. Therefore the planes number twelve, six astral and six heavenly. The last mental plane marks the stopping place or the ' Nirvana ' where the soul meditates, contemplates and absorbs the experiences of its past. This is the resting place after every incarnation before the soul returns to gather fresh experience.

Beyond these mental planes awaits—we will not call it the ' Third death '—but the final liberation from incarnation; for the soul then goes onward through the ' Waiting Halls ' into the celestial or cosmic consciousness.

CHAPTER II

THE HARMONY, PERFECTION
AND GLORY OF THE HEAVEN LIFE

'From the very beginning have ye been immortal and children of life.
—Valentinus.

'Thine own consciousness, shining, void, and inseparable from the Great Body of Radiance, hath no birth or death.
—Tibetan Book of the Dead.

'O Thou Who art light, truth, and love, the supreme and illimitable power of the universe; Thou Who art in the sweetness of every flower that blooms; in every human love that throbs in the heart of man; in the wind-swept sky, in the rolling waves; Who art indeed the breath in the heart of man. O Thou Who art our Father God, we bow before Thy majesty in thanksgiving for Thy love. May we be purified according to Thy desire, so that we become servants to Thy will. So may we live in the eternal with Thee. Amen.'

I

WHEN I left my body I found that I could not free myself from the entanglements of earth for a considerable period, yet it is impossible to describe the exact 'geography' of my position. I felt strangely linked with the place of my birth and early years, so that I could not escape either to return nor yet to advance to that heavenly plane which I knew existed, and must be quite near. Truly I was tied, and all my hopes of communicating with my friends were frustrated. I tried and tried again, and yet again, and found any contact most difficult. I was at a loss to understand the cause. I found myself able to give thought-projections, and sketchy bits seemed to filter through the denseness

105

around me. Slight messages such as these gave assurance to my family that I was conscious, at all events.

And then I seemed to be picked up, as it were, by a ray of light. A power unknown came to my aid, giving me understanding of my true state, and I subsequently learned that this ray of light was a projection of love and power from the Polaire Brotherhood. It proved of inestimable value to me and brought a clear vision of the actual state of life which exists immediately after death.

For it seems that every soul must pass through such a condition, or such a period of time, which may be short or long according to the mental condition of the man when he leaves his body. With some souls this is only a matter of a few hours or days; with others it may occupy years. Even the Master Jesus descended into a condition of uncertainty which is called Hades, the sphere of the disquieted spirits.* So also must every soul on leaving the earth pass through that sphere. As I have said before, it is very difficult for the soul to escape from its physical, mental and astral attachments—only the enlightened soul can traverse rapidly the spheres of the denser astral.

In spirit-life time ceases to have reality. ' In the twinkling of an eye we shall be changed '—as St. Paul said—' at the last day '—but this does not mean at the end of this world, as our Christian friends are apt to declare. It means at the end of the soul's *world of matter*; and the astral worlds are still worlds of matter, albeit of finer matter. Then, when the man passes through the grey astral spheres and is touched by the light of the eternal spirit of God, in the twinkling of an eye he is changed, and casts off the old terrestrial body and puts on the body celestial and dwells in the heart of eternal spirit. Truly, it is said that a gulf is fixed between the man who dwells in Abraham's bosom and the rich man imprisoned in the fires of hell! Can this be obviated? Will this same gulf always exist between the man of heaven and the man of earth? Always; that is, so long as the latter thinks only earthly thoughts and so houses his being in earthliness.

---

* ' He descended into hell; the third day he rose again.'

WE have dealt with the conditions immediately following death, and it may appear that we have enlarged overmuch on the gloomy side, by talking rather pessimistically about the grey astral spheres, the astral memories and the mistakes of the Spiritualists. This may be because I have so recently passed through that state, which is so disquieting and disturbing that it may have left a rather deep impression on that part of me which more readily contacts the earth.

The difficulty is to find adequate words with which to describe the conditions of life after death. The representations of life spent on the astral planes made from time to time through Spiritualism are often only the actual experiences of souls still closely linked with the earth. For on the astral planes are many conditions closely attuned to the desires of those dwelling there, much as on earth you get the many grades of society living in their own environment. You will therefore obtain a variety of descriptions, each appertaining to its own particular plane of astral existence. After passing through a ' death' of his astral body, when the man discards his astral vehicle and enters the heavenly life, we find at last a condition of at-one-ment, of attunement; a condition wherein the soul is conscious only of the one vibratory note of love and service permeating its being. In these spheres the soul thus becomes cognizant of the cosmic powers which rule creation.

WHEN speaking of the Second Death through which every soul must some day pass before it quits the astral, and after experiencing a period of unconsciousness which may last for minutes, hours, days or even years, we said that the soul then wakes to a renewed, rich and vivid life. Time is nothing over here, although we have to speak in terms of your earth time. The Second Death has taken place, and all that remained which was of the earth, earthy, in that soul has passed away. With the Second Death there comes the great awakening—the soul's awakening—when it sees truth revealed, and for a moment gains a vision of the mighty salvation attainable through Christ.

With such prospect as this in view the man advances into the *mental* condition of his being. I would, however, make it clear that the soul does not pass through every mental plane of the spiritual life, but automatically migrates to the particular mental plane to which it is attuned. Thereafter in succession the soul will work its way up through every plane or grade of *spiritual* existence; and this is not because of the single existence on earth which it is supposed each man undergoes (and thinks of as his only mortal life) but by and through every incarnate life which he has ever experienced. For the soul of each man lives through many incarnations. During each separate incarnation it will mark out the plane or place on the mental plane to which it will some day travel, and where it will for a period dwell. Thus, in the course of time that soul will experience every phase and every condition of the spiritual life.

Is this clear? Do you understand that during his life in the physical world man is always laying a foundation for the particular astral, mental, or celestial home to which he must go; so that he will attain a lesser or fuller degree of freedom and happiness in his astral, mental or celestial life in exact accordance with the degree of his aspirations and spiritual growth during his span on earth?

II

I HAVE now to endeavour to show the difference between the *mental* planes (whereon the soul emerges to dwell after the Second Death), the mental activities on these planes and the *celestial* life which lies beyond. For the mental body which man inhabits after quitting his experience in the astral worlds is a purely *mental* state, which differs widely from the spiritual state beyond.*

---

* The Chart of the ' Spheres of Evolving Life and Consciousness ' given on the opposite page originally appeared in *Thy Kingdom Come* as a double-page illustration in colour. It forms, of course, merely a diagrammatic explanation, and thus can give no idea of the interrelation of the spheres as they exist in the human consciousness—which is the reason why man lives in more worlds than one. Nevertheless it can be of use to the reader in distinguishing the several spheres, provided it is not thought of as an actual picture.

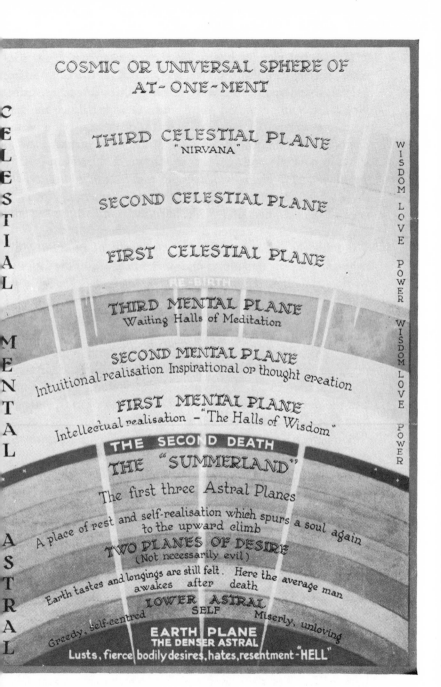

COSMIC OR UNIVERSAL SPHERE OF
AT~ONE~MENT

THIRD CELESTIAL PLANE
"NIRVANA"

SECOND CELESTIAL PLANE

FIRST CELESTIAL PLANE

REBIRTH

THIRD MENTAL PLANE
Waiting Halls of Meditation

SECOND MENTAL PLANE
Intuitional realisation Inspirational or thought creation

FIRST MENTAL PLANE
Intellectual realisation – "The Halls of Wisdom"

THE SECOND DEATH
THE "SUMMERLAND"

The first three Astral Planes

A place of rest and self-realisation which spurs a soul again
to the upward climb

TWO PLANES OF DESIRE
(Not necessarily evil)

Earth tastes and longings are still felt. Here the average man
awakes after death

LOWER ASTRAL
SELF

Greedy, self-centred   Miserly, unloving

EARTH PLANE
THE DENSER ASTRAL
Lusts, fierce bodily desires, hates, resentment "HELL"

CELESTIAL

MENTAL

ASTRAL

WISDOM LOVE POWER

WISDOM LOVE POWER

...HERES OF EVOLVING LIFE AND CONSCIOUSNESS

ACCORDING TO A.C.D.

The mental plane is one of great power, on which the soul must exercise its full mental faculties, which, as it were, become unleashed and augmented when it enters this plane of existence. Nor can it quit the mental plane until a delicate balance has been reached between its mental and spiritual qualities. For a period it would seem that the soul must remain on the mental plane to grow in quietude, much as a seed is sown in the soil and left to germinate. Having passed into the mental world, man has to dwell there to obtain soul-growth before emerging into the celestial world, bringing with him the spiritual power and equipment he has gathered during his journey.

It is in the *celestial* world that the work of creation really begins. That is the glory and magnificence of the celestial world, and of its creative art which is the real *becoming* of all creation. In this heaven world the soul of man absorbs a potency from the divine quality of Christ; having itself become almost angelic, it dwells among angelic beings sharing their lustre. Would that we could endow you with some flash of intuition or insight which would reveal a glimpse of the harmony, the perfection and the glory of this heaven life! For it is here that the soul of man becomes conscious at last of its true nature, here that the ego knows itself a very part of God.

After their passing from earth life the souls of men reach this celestial sphere of being in about thirty years of time (as men gauge time) and in the normal course of their development. Nothing drives the soul onward against its own inclination. Man's own power of freewill is ever operative. If he wants to linger in the astral conditions, he can stay as long as he desires, so that a century or more may pass; or if he wishes he can sometimes pass quickly onwards, but only when he is longing with all his heart to become re-united with the God-consciousness which is his real home.

What can it mean to such a soul to relinquish everything, willingly to renounce its heaven world in order to retrace its steps earthwards to serve men? To understand you would first have to conceive a tithe of the wonder and harmony of the heaven life. Yes, there are forms there which one sees as angelic, perfect in their beauty, with faces most tranquil and peaceful, and shining with the glory of a great peace and love. Each mind there is softened, serene, and has become beatified. The air we breathe is shining, rare and fine. The harmony of a divine music breathes continually within the soul, which finds its supreme joy in some form of service, some form of self-giving. For you must not conceive this heaven world as a sphere of idleness or perpetual rest, although it is a place of eternal peace; for it is by dwelling in such peace as this that we learn something about the ways of creation, and in so learning we become ourselves creative.

Yes, there are souls among *us* who willingly sacrifice such joys as these to descend again to the lower planes of earth to labour there. Like a diver descending to the deep, or a collier to the bowels of the earth, so can the descending soul, donning its astral garb, take on itself something of the limitations of a personality again. Even then it can labour in those lower spheres only for a period, for it must ascend again, as it were to breathe, unable to sustain for too long so dense an atmosphere.

Is it possible for souls dwelling in these celestial spheres to communicate from there with the earth? Yes. There are messengers for that very purpose. Few people understand the wonderful mysticism of parts of the Bible, as when Jacob dreamed he saw a ladder placed between heaven and earth, and saw angels descending and ascending it. People will perhaps regard this as a childish story. Yet that is just what is still happening. Communications are indeed coming down from the heaven world to the earth people: alas, that so much is lost in transit and that so much confusion exists concerning the right methods of communication!

We have spoken before about St. Paul's words: *In the twinkling of an eye we shall be changed*, and *When the last trump shall sound!* This means the great call which comes forth from the Supreme, from the Christ heart, to which all men shall some day find they are related. For soon or late each and every soul must awaken to that call, hear that peal of the trumpet of the spirit which is summoning it homewards. Men will then leave behind all that was of the earth, earthy, in themselves. By this surrender all their individuality will be preserved and enhanced, and their lower personality die and be shed. Do not regret it; for although personality is of the earth and soiled by earth it has yet been a means to an end, a means necessary if man is to undergo experiences which are invaluable on his upward climb to God.

Yes; teach the people about communion with the spirit world, but for God's sake teach them the truth. Do not offer them a fool's paradise by telling them that everything will be lovely there. I can assure you that the life after death is a serious matter, not to be regarded lightly, not a subject to be glossed over as with a varnish paint. For when a man passes from his physical to an astral condition he has to face the fruits of his past life on earth. There can be no more backsliding then, for life has to resolve itself into a forward march.

Proofs—what are these proofs that the people of the earth cry out for? They do not know what constitutes proof of the after-life. They only consider something that is capable of being conveyed to any of their five physical senses as proof of spirit power; and yet the great proof, the proof there is no gainsaying is manifesting itself in a very definite and drastic manner all over the face of the globe.*

III

LET us return to a further description of the mental plane, which is not to be confused with the celestial. Although these terms may appear baffling, the several planes in the mental world must be clearly subdivided. Thus, after the Second Death, the soul enters first a mental plane where it finds itself surrounded by the previous creations of its own mind. It is here that the chief characteristics of the man of cold, hard, intellectual thought

---

* The last sentence seemed incomprehensible at the time, but the proof of the existence of a spiritual law has since been demonstrated. For in these years which preceded the outbreak of war in 1939 the nations were surely sowing the seeds of war by reason of sloth, selfishness, godlessness. The war when it came was a demonstration of how certainly, how speedily spiritual laws operate even in the material world.

have found expression. The delicate balance which exists between the intellectual and the intuitional part of man must now be taken into account, for on the next or second mental plane the soul responds to the intuitional or spiritual light which is now drawing it upwards and onwards, ever higher and nearer to the central focus of its being, which is the Godhead. On this second mental plane the man becomes conscious of an intuitional inflow which tones down his hard intellectuality and enforces a purer intuitional conception of existence. In this condition the man himself becomes creative, since from this plane springs all the creative urge or activity which takes an ultimate form on earth as art, literature, music, religion, science, all of which are varying expressions of creative energy derived from a higher source: here, in short, man finds himself able to contact the Source of all his higher inspiration and creation. From this intuitional (but still mental plane, you understand) he passes to the higher, the third and last mental plane. Now he enters a state of quiescence.

For, as the man journeys upwards, he is ever shedding the vestiges of that stratum of himself which is of the earth, earthy; but absorbing the lessons he learns on his journey, lessons which are retained by his ego and become a part of himself. When the man attains the condition of quiescence, peace and tranquillity on the intuitional plane (which is not mere lethargy), his spirit remains perfectly conscious, although mentally in a state of soliloquy, able at last *to see himself as he really is*; to gauge the complete effect of his life, not only as it has affected the lives of his fellows on earth, but in relation to the whole creative principle; to estimate the magnitude or otherwise of his personal contribution towards God's evolving Plan of Creation.

THE third mental plane is a condition of withdrawal from outer form into an inner relationship with the universal power; a condition where man's inner ego contacts that universal sphere of spiritual being and attainment. Whereas life on the planes below has been in definite form, now there is *to some extent* an absence of form. It will be very difficult for the man of earth to imagine such a condition, concerned as he is with his form-life. When you attempt to visualise or imagine the Universal, that great Omnipotence whom you worship and love as God, your mind cannot conceive Him in any particular form; yet within your being and outside in the whole universe at all times and in all places, God's pulsating life radiates power—the effect of which you recognise by its myriad manifestations as an Intelligence ever proclaiming its handiwork. When you pray, you pray to a Mind that understands *your* mind, to a Heart that loves and is compassionate to *you*. It is nevertheless utterly impossible to formulate that Mind or Heart. For this reason the Cosmic Christ manifested as a man on the earth, that he might give form or provide a nexus, in order that men and women might make contact, according to their capacity, with the Godhead.

So when we reach the third mental plane we find absence of form: that is, man's ego is no longer limited, confined or bound down to any particular form of being, to any particular kind of body. He is rather spending his time, not only in withdrawal into the centre of himself, but also in expansion from that centre until his being contacts the whole, the life universal.

It is true that it is possible for men and women still living on earth to contact this sphere; but the effect is so powerful, the plane so tremendous in its vibration, that the effect can even be harmful to the human organism.

We touch on a vast theme. You have occasionally seen advanced souls living in your midst at whom men wonder; yet for some unknown reason a sudden collapse and death awaits them. They sometimes die of a disease which the medical world cannot diagnose. Again we say that until medicine deigns to study the laws governing man's spiritual being it will continue to be confronted and baffled by obscure diseases. Do not mistake us; we do not mean to convey that every one who dies from an obscure disease is necessarily of high spiritual consciousness whose end was due to contact with this third mental plane!

It has seemed necessary, however, to explain that this universal power can shatter man's body, unless it is sought in humility and truth, and with a pure and selfless motive. You will ask what is meant by this? We reply that within us all lies an inmost centre of our being, a divine birthplace of man's spirit, which even to reach, much less to comprehend, is beyond all intellectual striving or attainment. If a man attempts to reach this power by intellect alone, without due attunement, without growth of the spirit, there must inevitably be disaster. Yet if that same man will strive with mind and heart and spirit to seek the kingdom, holding fast in simple and childlike faith, he must reach that plane of the universal and there receive truth and power and life from the fount of all life.

We repeat, my friends, that on this third heavenly plane there is a withdrawal from expression through man's outer form into his inmost depths, and that in such withdrawal there must follow expansion and absorption into the universal life. With this the question will immediately arise: has such a man forever sunk his individuality and shed all traces of desire for evermore? No, my friends, no; the man has then become greater, nobler, with his individuality enhanced. Having tasted at last of the divine fruit, being at last aware of his own inherent divinity, he has become *at-one* with God, even as the Gentle One once said, ' *My Father and I are one.*'

Even then, the man can still return to earth. Although his ego has become like a seed deeply sown or embedded in the life-more-abundant of which Jesus spoke, his ego can emerge again, assume a form and step by step re-enter its former state of being, until if the man so desires he takes mortal life on himself once more.

IV

I HAVE spoken of a period of quietude where the soul reviews its past. This is before it passes onwards; for on those mental planes the man is more or less concentrating on *himself*, is labouring within himself, concerned now not so much with his *output* (as he had been on earth) as with his *intake* of truth regarding himself.

To cover the ground again: we have outlined three *mental* planes—i.e. the lower mental or intellectual; the intuitional; and the higher mental which contacts the cosmic forces. We then pass onwards to the true spiritual planes—the *celestial*. The Buddhists refer to this heavenly condition as nirvana, a term which well expresses that peace, that tranquil retracement by the soul of man over all the experiences it has gained.

Have you ever heard about the Waiting Halls of Heaven? Yes, there are such places; and the soul whose fulfilment is incomplete lives for a period in this mental state or plane, as a dweller in the Waiting Halls, having then gathered up its knowledge and reviewed all its past experiences both on earth and elsewhere. There the soul waits until the call comes for it to go forward, or else until it accepts the order to descend again into mortal life; to take another dip, as it were, much as a diver goes down into the sea.

WE have now referred in turn to the astral, the mental, the celestial, and the Christ spheres. There may have been some confusion of terms, and this is a matter I wish to clarify. After the astral and mental planes, then from the celestial we pass to what has been referred to as the Christ sphere, but which I desire to name henceforth the *cosmic or universal sphere*. In this condition of heavenly life dwell great Beings which are freed from rebirth on any physical plane of existence, and which are now concerned not only with the earth life but with all life, with the life of the universe. From this plane creative masters are sent forth, responsible for the life of the souls of lesser beings dwelling on other planets and in other spheres of existence.

Thousands of years (I can only speak in terms of earth time) must elapse before the ego attains its full expression and development; and only after gaining all possible knowledge through physical existence does it pass beyond the Halls of Waiting, beyond even the celestial planes into a still higher plane. What term can prove adequate for this? The Christ sphere . . . the place of at-one-ment with Christ . . . the rapture of love perfected, of perfect fulfilment which is found—yes, even these are waiting for the perfected soul of man.

When in transit between the mental and celestial spheres the soul becomes conscious of a spiritual element which it lacked before. This is due to its closer contact with the Christ sphere, from which the creative ones, the exalted ones, may descend to merge themselves into an earthly existence, to take on themselves mortality by supreme sacrifice. This is what happened when the Master Jesus made his renunciation—but you have yet so much to learn concerning his life and death.

It is unnecessary for man to pass through physical death in order to contact all the planes of spiritual life. This is knowledge vital to the being and happiness of every man. For man has power to reach out, to contact, and to respond to the influences which emanate from all the planes of spiritual being even while enmeshed in the flesh; the difference being that when he is released his spiritual life gains a sweet intensity. Having lost a physical body, the more surely does the soul-experience which he now undergoes afford him a richer and greater sense of reality in his being. Again and again we say that all the spheres of spiritual life are, or can be, reached by incarnate man, who can thus draw his experiences either from a hell of desire or a heaven of ecstasy.

CHAPTER III

THE SPHERE OF REUNION

' *Immeasurable Might, Ineffable Love! Great Architect of the Universe, we worship before Thy Throne of Grace. We come before Thee in humility, duly prepared to receive Thy commands. O Great One, take our will and make it Thine. Beautify our vision according to Thy truth. Inspire our minds with Thy goodness and make our hearts subject to Thee . . . O Thou Divine Love! Amen.*'

AT this stage of our discourse this question will arise: you will be thinking that all this is very interesting, but what about that vibrant human love and prospect of reunion with those who have gone before, which for so long has been our dream and longing—will this be ours in the spirit lands? What is the use, you will say, of becoming a formless mass of consciousness in those heavenly lands, like an egg without a shell? The prospect seems uninviting, when we have dreamed of love reunited, of love deep, rich and full, the fulfilment of which can alone make our earth life worth the price we pay for living it.

Yes, we too have had our sorrows; we too remember the yearning with which man looks forward to reunion, together with the attainment of a deep peace and happiness which the world can neither give nor take away. Men long have dreamed that beyond the River Jordan they might find reunion:

> And with the morn those angel faces smile
> Which we have loved long since and lost awhile.

Are we indeed destined to enter into some formless condition and to live in it for ever? No, I can assure you that there is indeed a special sphere in the spirit world, an almost heavenly place in the upper astral regions, far more beautiful than the

Summerland of the Spiritualist, a sphere where souls unite once more. Mark, this is a place for *the reunion of all grades of human life*, which includes any incarnate souls which can soar thither from the earth. It is the sphere (or place) of family reunions, which might be described as family gatherings, where all souls which are bound one to another by living and vibrant love can meet and greet one another. Note, however, that these reunions do not necessarily continue for overlong. We on this side and you on yours have duties to which we must all return when the call comes. Ours may be joyful; yours you may think of as sullen, grinding and laborious. Nevertheless men in all grades of life have to return to the particular condition or environment to which they are suited or to which they have adapted themselves.

There are periods of festivals in the astral world, much as you might celebrate a special birthday or anniversary, or the Christmas, Easter and Whitsun festivals. On these occasions folk meet in love, happiness and peace in order to exchange experiences. Yes, indeed a man from the earth can find his own beloved waiting for him, and dwell together in the happiness of a wonderful reunion. There also the people meet in massed concourse, in vast—no, not halls or temples—in vast open-air cathedrals where they praise God by song, and by love and prayer express their profound thankfulness.

Would you like to question me about this sphere of reunion? Ask if you wish, but refrain from discussing the matter between yourselves as this will cause confusion.

Question: *Suppose one partner follows another to the life beyond, and is much lower in spiritual attainment than the first, and so cannot reach the plane of reunion; what happens then?*

The person who has the higher spiritual quality can always raise the other, if only for a brief period. Illustrate this by your own experience. Take a woman of a deeply spiritual nature who greatly loves a man whom you might think unworthy of her. Can she not raise him, if only for a time, by her very presence and influence? It may be but a fleeting experience, but he will know that he has been near her for a flash. The same law operates in the spiritual worlds. Time is nothing over here; all is but a question of human consciousness; by *intensity of experience* two souls may live a period in a moment and the time seem long. A light will then have dawned on the struggling younger soul, and afterwards he will strive with added zest to reach again that plane of consciousness where some marvellous moment of blissful reunion was lived.

There can be no separation in spirit—no separation. Do you understand the implication of this? It must be very difficult, but try to get this idea of spiritual affinity; for although there may be work to be accomplished by the two on different planes of life, there is always *one* point at which loving souls may find their contact, although possibly only at given intervals. At times you yourselves can reach a high spiritual range of consciousness. True, you may fail to sustain your contact and fall, as it were, with a crash. Nevertheless you have had your moment. Surely to go to the spirit land for a space cannot be expected to make a man into an angel for ever?

How can I even make you understand the love and bliss souls here experience when at last they reach their beloved? What joy it is to know that separation—a real and sad separation—can never again be their lot; although they must perforce sometimes go their separate ways to service and to labour. With what relief must they realise that separation as they once knew it has died forever in the arms of love!

Question: *What of twin souls who are indeed affinities? What is their destiny?*

This is a big question, but here again there is no question of two souls (or twin souls) merging into one individual, or of the individuality of either becoming absorbed in the other, or both in one; but there may develop such perfect harmony of desire and understanding between the two that the two life-courses run as one within a single channel. When souls reach the higher spheres both their active and passive aspects still remain; in other words, they are still man and woman; and each will continue to contribute his or her particular creative ray of life-force to the universal.

I want to emphasise this truth again and again. With the eternal and absolute God there can never be any question of absorption; and yet it is all absorption. Here is a paradox—but do you not see? In becoming *one* you become a part of *all*; in becoming *all* you must become *one* with God. This is a magnificent and transcendent thought. Could man only grasp, if only momentarily or occasionally, some faint glimmer of this truth, world affairs might take a mighty turn for the better. World friction would cease because man would be translating himself from the *personal* point of view to a realisation of his true nature. It was to this that Jesus Christ strove to awaken men.

While we are here we would leave yet another thought to mature in your minds. On the plane of consciousness we have called the universal, which means the allness of all life, man can control the elements, and create at will by filling his consciousness with the universal creative life-force. This is the secret of which the Masters make use; by operating in accord with that universal vibration they overcome (or rather control) all the material elements around them. With equal facility they control not only the material but the astral and mental elements in their respective spheres.

It can be done by a Master who can by an effort of his spiritual will-power (not the will-power of his physical mind) raise and so quicken his vibrations as to attract the atoms of any of these differing planes to himself. When they have accumulated, he gradually lowers or slows them down until they become no longer spiritual but physical atoms, to be formed into whatever article or substance he desires.

Many people question the truth of the feeding of the five thousand people with five loaves and two fishes, asking how the Master Jesus could accomplish this miracle. It was done by raising his consciousness to the Universal, by holding his thought *at-one* with God, and by thus attracting to that thought the spiritual atoms, slowing them down, and determining what particular form of matter those atoms should take. Thus he fed the five thousand.

WE have spoken about the sphere of reunion, which in other words means a condition of spiritual understanding in which all souls can meet. We have mentioned the family reunions which take place there. We have tried to show that even from the earth life this ' common ' plane, sphere, or condition of spiritual harmony and contact can be reached. In preceding talks it has been indicated that the life which man thinks of and calls ' the life after death ' is in reality *the life of his eternal spirit*; so that these realms of spiritual consciousness cannot be limited to the life discarnate but are open to man always—yes, are open to you here and now.

This is a crucial point; this more-abundant-life of man's soul and spirit, erroneously thought to exist only after death, is the life of his past, of his present and his future. It is in fact a portion of the life eternal in which man lives; the life which every soul is living and contacting every moment, no matter whether he is housed in a fleshly body or functions on any plane of the spiritual realms.

Recognition of the reality of this inner spiritual life will some day harmonise and unify every school of thought, every religion which holds the hearts of men. It is indeed the full ' gospel of universalism '.

CHAPTER IV

CONCERNING NATURE-SPIRITS AND ANGELS

' *Great Architect of the Universe, we assemble again with one accord to receive from Thy Ministers divine truth of life and being. We, Thy servants, being duly prepared, present ourselves before Thee, waiting Thy commands; and we remember that with Thy wisdom in our hearts, Thy beauty in our vision, and Thy will in our hands we may go forward to complete Thy work in Thy Name to Thine honour and glory for ever and ever. Amen.*'

NEITHER brush nor pen can depict the beauties of the heaven world. Man can only glimpse faintly the wonders of the spiritual life which await him, and few there are who either by aspiration or by actual contact with high spiritual spheres can catch fleeting visions of their glories. These are the real artist and true writer, the musician, the poet and the man of fervent religion. But even their glimpses of heaven cannot be sustained and must fade when the man returns to mundane affairs.

It is true; the spirit world and the physical are inextricably interwoven, so that it is impossible for man to separate the two states of his being. But when he has advanced to a degree of understanding which enables him to comprehend this, then his own mortal world will not seem so dense, so material to him. So also when men in the mass grasp these things will their world become more refined, more ethereal; and men will enter into what is more like an astral than their present physical condition. Such a future as this will unfold itself. Even in your day this gradual etherealisation of the physical atom will begin, and the earth will become progressively more beautiful as humanity advances on the path of its spiritual evolution.

HERE we will pause and touch upon another aspect of life which hitherto has been much neglected—that is, on the natural or nature-spirit line of evolution. Hitherto we have been concerned only with human life, incarnate and discarnate, to the exclusion of nature. We must now take into account the life of the plant, of the animal, the life existing in the elements, which are all planes of pulsating life-force distinct from the human. Let us remember that nature also continues into other worlds, and that its ordered evolution or plan of existence includes the astral, the mental and the celestial planes. But natural life seems to fit into the plan of creation in a more perfect and orderly manner than does the human. Strange as it may seem, I have always been a follower of the ' little folk ', and have loved the fairy tales which delight children—fairy tales as they seem to the hard-headed person, but actually the most delightful little realities one could imagine.

I now take much joy in visiting the great underworld—shall I call it the wide undergrowth?—of nature life; much joy in watching the little gnomes and fairies at work in the gardens of the earth, and on higher planes, happily weaving dreams and aspirations into a scene of beauty some day perhaps to be captured by an artist or writer dexterous with brush or pen; in watching the little people busily creating *their* representations of the divine love and beauty of God.

All this may perhaps sound rather too flowery, and doubtless you will expect us to come down to more practical and concrete descriptions of the nature life. We continue and can but do our best.

How sensitive is this plant world about us ! How wonderful it is to see the little fairy creatures busily carrying life-force and sustenance to the plants ! Lacking this fairy aid your plants would soon wither and die. Without plant life man would soon die likewise. Without the major powers controlled by the lords of nature, by the devas, your physical world would fall into chaos. Man speaks and thinks complacently of a law and order which automatically functions to govern his universe, but without seeking any deeper understanding of the mighty spiritual power which holds the sun and planets on their courses. The religious man speaks trustingly of a Divine Plan and of a loving Father Who orders all things aright; but he fails to take into account the marvellous organisation existing in the spiritual spheres for the control, retention and maintenance of the law and order he sees in nature.

Men of science are apt to regard these happenings as a normal part of material existence by reason of laws which they name but can never understand. They affirm that if a seed be planted in the earth and given certain conditions of moisture, sunshine and warmth, the seed will become a plant. The rest of men accept this outcome, not as a miracle, not as a wonderful manifestation of divine power, but as a commonplace happening; much as collective man accepts the general routine of nature which supports him as a matter of course, and almost as a matter of right; thus refusing to pay tribute to that infinite care, love and patience which is the Causation of all.

Behind every manifestation of the life-force on the earth, the human included, broods the great world of Spiritual Reality. Truth and Love thus ever serve this world and the universe. I only wish that you, my friends, could some day open your inner sight as you walk in your garden, so as to see the innumerable little folk at work on your plants and flowers. Maybe they would seem to ignore you, but then they are all busily building, busily active in creating their part of the life of earth.

I catch a thought—yes; there are indeed angels in touch with this earth who have evolved not through the human but through the *nature* line of progress. It is true that some of them sometimes become attached to the human race in order that they may impart certain knowledge, or bring an addition of power or accomplishment to some person whom they serve. For instance, angel beings are attracted to religious services where ceremonial is practised—this is no fairy tale; I am giving you facts, for I have myself seen angels present during ceremonial or sacred functions. Some more or less nebulous knowledge concerning the Angels of Life and Death has also filtered through. Maybe you will regard these angels as evolved souls which were once of the human race? You are wrong. An Angel World exists apart from the human race, apart from the human chain of evolution, formed of souls which have never incarnated in a human body; of souls which have advanced through their own process of natural development, and which are in close accord with laws of creative service which benefit all creatures. Of such are the Angels of Music. (Here I would interrupt my theme for a moment to compare the ' little people ' with the ' little tones ' of music which in the aggregate form a mighty union or diapason, and swell out as a sublime harmony of nature.)

There will come a time, friends, when the brotherhood of men and of angels will be better understood. To such an end as this the whole of creation and evolution labours that it may bring about complete understanding and harmony between all of God's creatures.

Why not? You are one, and we are one—all is united in reality. Man will realise this when he has passed the Second Death, and is reborn to a realisation which dawns and afterwards grows within him for evermore; reborn to that expansion of consciousness which realises once and for all that in the giving and serving of his brothers and sisters in all kingdoms of life the man becomes at-one with the Universal. Within that understanding the soul grows to become at-one with God, and loses itself only to find in its submission Christ the Lord.

Do not imagine that any one plane of existence, be it of nature, or of the astral, mental or heaven worlds is spaced far above man somewhere in an illimitable heaven. All of them are waiting to be found within your own consciousness. Nearer are they than breathing to man. The one lesson we all have both to absorb in our hearts and live out in our lives is that *the kingdom of heaven is within.*

It requires no great intellectualism to enter that kingdom, but only the simplicity of heart of a little child. So tell and teach your own children about the fairies. Look for them yourself in your garden, and then hold communion with the universal life of nature of which they are a part.

Here then is my last thought—*simplicity*; that is the keynote, simplicity. Life is not complex. Only the ignorant themselves—a sweeping statement but true—make it complex. Life is great in its simplicity and simple in its greatness. That is all.

CHAPTER V

FREEWILL AND DESTINY—BOTH EXIST

'The Father of Life, of existence—through Whom all acts and
breathes . . . Whose Wisdom has meditated the excellence of
all that exists.'

—The Popal Vuh.

WE have already disassociated ourselves from the idea that the
spheres of spiritual life are concerned solely with life after death.
This is not so. Instead, we have explained how the influence
of these spheres interpenetrates both the astral and the physical
planes. Indeed, we cannot sever these spheres from the physical;
and this is a most important lesson yet to be learned by man.

We would refer you to our talk about life in the nature
kingdom, when we spoke of the marvellously intricate life of
the nature spirits; and of the rhythmic harmony and attunement
existing between all grades of being in the natural kingdom.
Compare these marvels with the far more wondrous ray of
cosmic life and being which penetrates and interpenetrates every
aspect of man's being; and then try to realise the splendour of
the love with which the Father God would endow every one
of His children.

You little realise, my friends, as you go your daily way, how
marvellously you are guided and cared for at every step by unseen
helpers and friends; whose labours on your behalf you take as a
matter of course—even if you are aware of them. We speak of
the guides who come down to care for the human soul, and
labour sometimes for years and even for a life-time to produce
some spark of divine light within the soul's consciousness.
Undaunted, they persist, constantly endeavouring to piece
together the broken fragments and disharmonies of human lives,
to awaken in the human soul some degree of the Christ-consciousness. While they labour continually with humanity on

the earth they also descend to labour *beneath* your earth on the dense astral planes; as they do on the higher astral as well. From the lowest rung of the human ladder of existence to the highest this transcendent love and care for the human soul is exercised. At this point you will ask where a man's power of freewill choice comes in; how are we to be judged—by the measure of our desires, of our achievements, of our failures? For if this same mighty power is exercised even over the outer framework of man's daily life, surely we are no more than pawns or puppets in the great game? This is not so, my friends. Although this care over the inner life of man has been ordained by the great Lord of Love it does not detract by one iota from man's power of freewill choice of action.

For indeed you are continually making choices; continually deciding whether you will follow the upward or the lower path; whether you will be positive or negative in your reactions to events, constructive or destructive. Only, should you choose to follow the lower then you must needs experience the *effect* of your choice, of your decision, through undergoing suffering and tribulation.

Freewill exists, and so does destiny. And here we are brought face to face with our problem of *freewill versus destiny*—and what a mighty and seemingly insoluble problem it is! How little is it understood! Yet how little can it be understood until it is realised that man can only find a solution to these problems (of which there are many) through his gradual growth into knowledge of God, and never by straining his physical intellect. For man both destiny and freewill choice exist.

Destiny, so far as the individual man is concerned, stands for a range of physical experiences through which he must and will pass in the course of his mortal life; freewill choice lies *in his own reaction spiritually* to the series of conditions, the environment or circumstances which constitute and largely rule his ordinary physical life. If these reactions make him sweeter and kinder in nature, then life will grow gentler with him. If they embitter him, making him harsh and ruthless with his fellows, then he will attract harsh happenings to himself—according to the law of cause and effect, which he thus brings into operation.

We pause to consider that power of God which interpenetrates every moment of our life and being; to consider again the wonderful organisation which exists and rules the natural kingdoms and the creative life in all nature, forever encouraging and unfolding the life of the plant, bird, beast and man. Consider again that same creative force which without deviation holds the stars on their courses in the heaven; and which is ever causing birth and life, death and re-birth—in a sequence of life and death which runs like a rhythmic wave throughout all creation. Then ask yourself if you, if any of us can conceive even a tithe of the power of that Infinite Intelligence which creates this indomitable life-urge, and having brought it into being, sustains it through aeons of time.

Then think again of our wonderful collective human life—indeed of your own individual human lives—of the power which supports you through all things, the power which is bringing *to you*—and also bringing you *through*—a series of physical-life experiences which are destined to weave some pattern of spiritual beauty and truth into the warp and woof of your inner being.

If you could glimpse for one moment those gracious and wholly beautiful beings who live so harmoniously and tranquilly in the celestial spheres; if you could see their beauty of face and form, it would bring some conception of the wondrous inflowing life of the Christ-consciousness which has been working through aeons of time and through many recurring lives eventually to produce beings of such radiance. Let it be remembered that every man is step by step being thus gradually trained and unfolded, so that he also is developing his own illimitable mastership and Godhead.

Think well, then; for every effort of man's mind, will and spirit, every action, every experience of his from the smallest to the greatest, goes to the creating of such a Man as this. Alas, when such realisations as these illumine one's understanding one is appalled . . . *appalled at the ingratitude and selfishness of one's own inconstant heart!*

CHAPTER VI

THE PROBLEM OF GOOD AND EVIL

' The nature and essence of the Good is a certain disposition of the Will; likewise that of Evil.'

—Epictetus.

' *Most high and perfect Spirit of the Universe, great Architect, we come before Thee praying that Thou wilt guide us in all our ways. May the wisdom of Thy mind inspire our work. May the beauty of Thy form be made manifest in our work; may Thy love inspire our every thought and action towards our fellows. May we pass through life's journey in safety, and come at last into Thy glorious Presence, perfected through Thee. Amen.*'

TONIGHT power seems to come with such dynamic force that I am almost swept off my feet, and could be driven like a straw before the blast. This seems a good simile for the power of the spirit which is poured down onto the earth at this time. In the course of this outpouring you will see both national calamities and international disturbance; but ultimately a rebuilding of humanity owing to this power of the spirit.

The same message was given to me during my earth life. I can but repeat it, and say there will be physical catastrophes. As a result a great new continent will emerge where there is now but a waste of ocean, and there will be an equivalent subsidence of land.

The fiat has gone forth; even now we can see these creative Powers at work. A race of men will evolve considerably in advance of the humanity of today. Together with these changes will come refinement of the physical substance of the earth itself, and of the spheres which surround it.★

★ No time factor is given for these happenings, which may lie in the distant future.

131

But this is a diversion. We now return to the subject of the planes above the astral; to the first mental, to the intuitional plane above it, and to the third plane of intelligence or wisdom. We have explained that Christian Science as a collective body draws its power from the first mental plane. On the next plane, the intuitional, there is withdrawal from the hard intellectual condition. On the third plane, where the influence of the first and second planes becomes perfectly balanced and merged, we arrive at a state of consciousness or intelligence which might be called divine wisdom.

We must differentiate between intellect, which conditions life on the first mental plane, and that wider consciousness which exists on the third mental plane which we call ' intelligence.' This is a very part of the Divine Mind. Very many men, alas, who are thought by their fellows to be clever and intellectual really lack intelligence. From this plane of divine intelligence or wisdom we can draw creative power, but not that power which produces *form* on the astral planes; the power which can produce an actual *substance*, as Jesus demonstrated in the story of the loaves and fishes.

On all the planes of being we have described dwell angels of light and angels of darkness. Can you grasp this fact with all its implications? Perhaps you have hitherto imagined that all the dark angels are flung down to exist in some pit of degradation, while the angels of light are raised to the highest heaven to sit at God's right hand? Nothing can be more erroneous than any such idea, which has for centuries falsified man's outlook on both good and evil. Tonight it is my mission to awaken men to the realisation that these dual armies of intelligent beings —or if you will, the angels of light and darkness—work and evolve side by side, and are necessary one to the other. This fact must be assimilated before any clear conception of the real nature of good and evil can dawn. Hitherto men have conceived that good must always oppose evil. Nothing is farther from the truth. Evil is always an essential complement to that quality or condition man calls ' good ', and without the existence of evil good could not evolve or exist.

Let us consider again the angels of light and darkness, realising that these two Powers labour hand in hand unceasingly
for the soul of man, in order to perfect in him that Divine
Intelligence which ever strives to manifest itself through all
varieties of form and substance. From every plane of spiritual
activity, including the third mental plane of meditation and
contemplation, this angelic work goes forward. From this third
plane can be drawn power, which, reaching the earth, can
penetrate down even to the lower forms of creation—much as
the rays of sunlight and sun-power descend upon the earth.
The lower the plane of existence, however, the less active is that
power from on high.

We have said that from all the planes of spiritual life and consciousness there can be drawn a power which can be and is being
utilised by men, either for good or ill. Never run away with
the idea that all spiritual power from on high must necessarily
be ' good ' or ' white '. What then of the Principalities and
Powers of Darkness, the Adversaries and Princes of the Shadow
spoken of by St. Paul, who being a disciple of the Ancient
Wisdom knew both good and evil at their true worth? We
can recognise many an instance of men and women utilising
such powers for their own selfish and evil purposes. Think
back, over the life-history of many a war-lord and conqueror,
many a financier who has enriched himself by beggaring other
men, if you want an example.

Are these ideas too difficult for you to accept at present?
Surely not. Take for example a man who becomes over-
anxious to acquire wealth in order to benefit himself. Once he
has attracted these powers to himself something within him more
forceful than his own will for gain drives him onward.
Eventually he reaches a state when despite his own longing to
stop money-grabbing he cannot, even if by now he loathes the
wealth which enslaves him. Control is lost; the money piles
up in an influx he is unable to arrest, although by now no man
knows better than he the burden and curse of wealth. Other
examples of this nature can be found in the successful writer,
the dramatist, the statesman, and indeed in any walk of life

where men lust for wealth or power. Beware lest the driver himself becomes the driven soul. Beware! The angels of darkness are at work!

If you wish you can trace out for yourselves the operation of this shadowing power overriding many a life which has ended in failure and disaster. Would it not be altogether better for the world if all evil could be destroyed for evermore, so that only good would remain? If such a happening as this is conceivable, would it be desirable? or would it end in disaster?

We ourselves cannot see that any such happening would make for a suddenly perfected world, but rather the reverse. Will it help if you visualise two great wheels, two rings, two cycles ever revolving one against the other, each holding and maintaining as it were by a magnetic force, the position of the other? Does this give any indication how Providence works towards the enlargement of man's soul, towards its harmonisation with the Divine?*

We would impress this on all people, were we able: *That which man calls 'evil' is also of God; the Universal Intelligence which man calls God contains in Itself both good and evil!*

I know that such a statement as this must create controversy. I can only give the truth as I know and see it to be. For each of us must labour and strive so to live that we attain a perfectly balanced life, so that darkness shall never overcome the light in us; but rather that good and evil shall together, not as masters but as our servants, work out in us the perfect law with perfect precision. At the present time there comes an overruling, an overshadowing of the world by the powers of darkness. The earth has to readjust herself, or to find again and maintain her moral balance, to strive after a balanced perfection which in itself is beyond good and evil. For it is ordained that good and evil shall become servants to man, even as they are now God's

---

* Here A.C.D. partially failed to get his meaning across in words; but by his gestures endeavoured to indicate two immense Cycles ever turning one against the other, ever in a perfect rhythm and by this rhythm maintaining the moral balance of the world, much as centrifugal and centripetal force keep a planet poised in the solar system.

servants helping to work out His perfect Plan. That is the ultimate. It is only when individual man is raised above his physical and personal thought-life that he can realise life as *one stupendous whole*; and see life revealed as one comprehensive ' allness of God ', wherein there is no enduring difference between good and evil, black and white.

At this some questioner will ask, ' If what you say is true, are we not robbed of all impetus towards good? What need is there for anyone to try to improve the world, or himself, if after all there is no real difference between right and wrong? We might just as well rub along in any old way, if everything is going to come right in the end.'

We remind you that as the stars are poised in the heavens so also is every human soul poised in the eternal cycle of life; is held there by and within the unsleeping consciousness of the Divine Intelligence. It is true that the soul has been given a measure of freewill, or power of choice, so that it can accept or reject good or evil; but it has no power at any time to sever its link with the Supreme Soul, God—*and there is always an upward pull towards God.* True enough, for a time the soul may deride, deny or reject God; but it can never escape from Him, never break its link with Him; and in its extremity it must surely yield to Him, and return to Him like the Prodigal Son in the parable.

What is happening while the soul is resolved to resist the pull of God which draws it upward? It means that by his own will the man chooses the downward instead of the upward path. Mark, he has not escaped from God, not even for a moment. The magnetic power of the Divine Intelligence ever holds fast, is ever inclining him to tread the path back to God. Yet through a myriad transgressions he will follow the path of evil, downwards, downwards. At last comes the inevitable change of heart, the arising, the beginning of the long upward climb with bleeding feet back to God. This is why no man can ever escape his destiny, which is to attain to ultimate perfection through an ultimate return to his Creator.

Yet it is true that before man can become godlike he must pass through the lowest arc, must bottom the depths of evil as well as attain the heights; must pass through the deepest hell and touch the high heaven which is his eventual home.

When the personal man can grasp a truth so tremendous as this he will cease to condemn any fellow creature; for then the bright ideal of man's perfect soul, towards which both he and all his fellow creatures are striving through good and through evil will fill his heart with gladness. He will then think, ' My brother's path is his choice alone; my path is mine. What matter? Why should I condemn anyone?' The human ego can attain by this path alone to mastership; first over its own weaknesses and failings, then over its environment and the many limitations with which human life is encompassed.

We are endeavouring to reach up to spheres of cosmic life which are above both the mental and celestial spheres we have described. From such spheres beings of the highest spiritual consciousness can ascend and descend, and are still able to maintain touch with mortal man. When a man by continual effort can get into touch with such beings he can receive clear communications from the inhabitants of other planets. Although man has long tried to invent an instrument in order to obtain such communications, he will eventually learn that only within his own inner self, interpreted by his own spiritual intelligence, can anything of the kind be established. First man must attain to brotherhood with his fellow-man in social and national life; and then to brotherhood between nations. Later will follow an interplanetary brotherhood, born of the interplanetary communication which will some day become possible when the consciousness of humanity is raised.*

First, however, we have to learn the basic elements of such brotherhood. Man cannot live by bread alone, but by every word which proceedeth out of the mouth of God. In other words man can only accomplish or attain to fullness of living through constant contact with spiritual truths.

We are well aware that our statements about the real nature

---

* It is worth recalling that this prediction of interplanetary communication was given some twenty years before the advent of space ships and ' saucers ' from other planets was reported.

of good and evil will evoke much criticism. Nevertheless we re-emphasise the fact that these two are not so opposed in nature as their appearance seems to warrant. Marching in step with the creative power of good must always tread the destructive power of evil. During his earth life man finds it essential to destroy or consume rubbish and garbage. So it is with the economics of the universe. Might we not describe the angels of darkness, therefore, as the individualised powers of evil, representative of great destructive forces which consume all that is unwanted in the scheme of existence in a process of perpetual absorption and destruction of things, habits, customs, of modes of thought and living, which have become out of date and undesirable?

You see, we are suggesting that the powers of evil come under a cloak which hides an ultimate goodness. Being themselves negative in nature they must absorb from life—from human and universal life—all that needs to be cast off or discarded. But while they appear to destroy, in reality they do not destroy; although we have said they consume, actually they *transmute*.

Let us conceive them as agents which are ever active transmuting all that is undesirable in our midst to the eventually useful and beautiful. Let us recall our idea of the two mighty cycles—shall we say of God's evolving Purpose or Plan?—which men call positive or negative, or, roundly, ' good and evil '. Each is the complement of the other; both are necessary to the scheme of creation of the absolute. As certainly as night follows day and day night, does evil balance good and good evil. This process of transmutation of good to evil, of evil to good is ever proceeding. In this fashion the great cycles roll onward through aeons of time, their eventual purpose being to help the soul of all humanity to attain perfect balance and perfect harmony. When attained at last, this perfect culmination always heralds yet another putting forth of God's energies for the creation of new worlds destined for the habitation of new races of men. The House of God is thus ever in process of enlargement to make ready for the Day when His children return from their wanderings in time and space.

These are only some of the reasons which make it utterly impossible for the finite mind ever to comprehend eternity. Again we can only help you by suggesting that eternity is best represented by the great wheel which is never checked, never halted on its course.

Yes, *God is both good and evil;* God contains both good and evil within Himself. It is only your conception of evil which is wrong. Therefore you must accept what we say. May we suggest that evil as man sees it is rather man's *thought-concept* of evil than its real self? If any person exists thinking only about satisfying himself and his desires, he lives a selfish one-pointed existence in a state of darkness which men call evil. If on the other hand, sparing nothing for himself, he lives and labours to help and serve his fellows in common brotherhood he then dwells in the light, and draws fresh light to himself by opening himself to the heaven world. Cannot you see that that which seeks either good or evil is merely a *reflection*, is only the outer or personal self of the real man; and that the inner man, made in God's image, knows that both are one and the same in that they serve God?

Man looks out at the world around him and seeing much ignorance, cruelty and evil asserts that it is impossible to deny the reality of evil. His conclusion is based on false premises. What possible means has any man of judging whether a fellow creature serves either good or evil? His opinion is largely based on the conventions of his age, or the customs of his particular country. What seems good at one time is often declared wholly evil by a later generation, or by people of another continent.

We have yet to speak of an order of beings seldom described, but I think they are usually known as angelic beings—'winged beings', the great devas whose powers hold the ordering of many lives;* who command such wondrous power that without it man's world would lack much of its fragrance and sweetness. I speak also of the angels of birth and of motherhood, and of

---

* The devas control the group-souls of the nature kingdom, of which ants and bees are a prominent example, but their powers extend beyond the insect to the vegetable, animal and bird life.

the kindly angels of death; of the angels of music, of art and literature. Does the creative artist ever dream that the emotions of which music, art and beauty are the outcome, that the vibrations which are so fine, so delicate, originate from spheres beyond the dull earth environment, from heights outside the compass of human mentality? All spiritual beauty must emanate from the heaven worlds and the heavenly beings inhabiting it. Yes, these winged angels are dual personalities crowned by the love borne one to the other and to the whole universe.

It is profoundly difficult to express spiritual realities with words fitted only to describe material and physical conditions. Nevertheless, I would hold out to all people a hope beautiful and true beyond compare. I would assure them of the progress to be won by man's constant desire for beauty, love and wisdom. I would describe a life perfect in its power to express all the higher feelings and attributes which lie hidden in the depths of man's nature. Not one soul, whether it be of a white, a black, a yellow or a red man, but finds provision made for it in the vast universe of spirit. I would paint such a picture of the heaven world, were I able, that it must satisfy every desire and fire the imagination of every living soul on earth. Were the words mine I would show a world of spirit ever evolving, opening to new vista after vista of beauty. As one attains one sees fresh heights beyond. The air grows finer, brighter. Exultation fills one's being, nerving one to fresh effort and attainment.

CHAPTER VII

'AT TIMES THE WHOLE PANORAMA
OF HUMAN LIFE OPENS BEFORE ME'

' Raise the stone and thou shalt find me; cleave the wood and I am there.'

—Reputed saying of Jesus.

' I saw how His omnipotence penetrated everything, and was the foundation of all things.'

—Komensky.

' The sensible fire is in everything, and passes through everything unmingled, and springs from all; and whilst all-luminous, is hidden, unknown, in its essential nature.'

—Dionysos the Areopagite.

I

WE have told you that every phase of life in the spiritual realms interpenetrates the plane of physical life, and that man while still in the body can be active on the astral, mental, and spiritual planes to which he will pass on leaving the earth. This brings us to the core of a real spiritual philosophy, and indeed of every religion which has ever been or ever will be; for the basic truth of all ancient religion lies in this teaching about the soul of man; and this not merely during its earth-existence, or even when it passes into the unseen, but during the whole course of its soul life, onwards from when it first became a separate ego, a projection from the great Sun of all Life. This teaching comes down from the very birth of time, when man dwelt in his highest form of consciousness, and before his descent into the depths of materialism, out of which he now struggles on the upward arc of his evolution. Yet through the ages which have been occupied in this descent, man has never been entirely bereft of an inner consciousness of his true being and his relationship with the Godhead.

The life of the spiritual realms represents always the inner life of man. In his *descent* from God it becomes less evident, since the life-urge is then a 'putting out' into bodily form, the formation of a personality with which to encounter the trials of material life; whereas in his *ascent* there comes a *withdrawing into*, a seeking-out and rediscovery of his own true nature and of the vast spiritual heritage which can be his.

I would emphasise again that during man's life on earth he is meant to acquire that quality of consciousness with which he can and does manifest on the numerous inner planes; so that when he is freed from the prison of flesh he will automatically migrate to the particular plane, to the particular world for which he has fitted himself. Do you not see that when man acquires this vision of his future, this knowledge of the purpose of his mortal life, his existence will become orderly; and he will no longer be the victim of mischance, or subject to accident, disaster or injustice in any form?

When people express loathing at the thought of any future reincarnation into a mortal existence, this indicates a closed mentality. It would seem that a shutter has come down on a section of their spiritual mind, as though a dark curtain hangs between the seeming outer realities that possess them and their own inner and deeper intuitive knowledge of reality. When one reviews life and examines closely the length of human experience which is necessary before the soul of man can draw near to its spiritual completion, one must recognise not only the necessity for man to incarnate again and again, but the tremendous importance of even the smallest detail in his life.

In the world of spirit everything is law, order and harmony. Few people will dispute that in the world of nature everything reacts to an exact law; and physical as these laws seem in their outworking, they all originate from the spiritual universe. There can be no haphazard methods, for nature is very drastic with delinquents. This also happens in the spiritual spheres where the smallest action calls forth an exact reaction. This means that man's thoughts become his creations, that they become like angels of good and evil to him; so that when he views his life from some higher plane of existence, he well realises the disastrous nature of those mental creations of his—of gloom, depression and selfishness—which were and are his mental children.

I touched on this earlier. This has affected me deeply since my arrival here, for I was wont to create such characters, scenes and word-pictures. Mine was a vivid imagination; and, while I gave forth many a picture of joy, homeliness and beauty, my pen also depicted scenes of crudity, ugliness, crime and horror. While recognising that such pictures may by their very contrast teach their lesson, on the other hand creations of ugliness and terror are apt to live on in men's minds, and fill them with violent and unhealthy vibrations. Now I gaze down into the lives of men and women who have been considerably influenced by me for either good or ill. This I tell you only to illustrate the lesson.

Some day every man will attain either the joy or the terror of seeing the effect of his creations, beautiful or the reverse; no matter whether they are merely fictitious characters or actual conditions of life resulting from actions of his which have considerably influenced the lives of others. He will then see his own personal contribution, be it of good or evil, to the collective whole: shall we not say ' positive ' and ' negative ' rather than good and evil? The positive vibration alone is the creative one, the eternal; while the negative, being the destructive force, must end in suffering and pain.

These are the reasons why man today begins to recoil from the sight of his sick and ailing world. Suffering must be the result of man's sowing of the very seeds of suffering. Yet we in the spirit can still see the rays projected from the great Sun of all Life. This is why evolution still swings on the upward arc; however strong the downward pull, there remains a still greater power of attraction; and humanity will yet be saved by a true instinct within itself, by its deep and innate hunger to return to God.

YES, we can promise the coming of a new heaven and a new earth, for the old earth is passing away; of a new heaven and a new earth because humanity is creating anew both heaven and earth by its striving after God. God's workmanship ever labours towards an unimaginable perfection in spite of resistance by ignorance, cruelty and wrong.

The old world passes, yet it will live again.

The same laws which rule on earth rule on each succeeding plane of man's being. In the degree that man on earth aspires to become godlike even as his Creator, and in the degree he opens to receive the divine love and power of God, so does his life among men raise the material vibrations of the whole globe on which he dwells. To the limited and circumscribed five senses that present-day man possesses, the etherealised world of the future would seem intangible, even invisible to some people. None the less it will embrace a greater measure of reality than anything this world of time and sense can at present produce. Planets of an ethereal substance are even now within the radius of the solar system; but they are invisible to the eye of man or to his most powerful telescope. They are so spiritualised as to have risen beyond the compass of physical vision.

While man remains in his present lowly estate he cannot recognise anything outside his own capacity. Like a fish swimming in muddy waters he gropes his way onward, unconscious that other spheres beyond death even exist. He is blind also to these more ethereal and beautiful planets in our solar system. This new universe, existing beside the physical, can only appeal to an enlarged and quickened consciousness. It is, by the way, distinct from the planes of the after-death state which interpenetrate the physical order.

The earth is the darkest planet of the system, so that all of you have a brighter future to which you may look forward. If only the people of earth would open their hearts to us, and let us dispel their fear of death, they might step more bravely forward on the road leading to beauty, wonderment, and joy of living.

As we have said earlier, worlds exist of which your astronomers know nothing, worlds composed of etheric matter, the influence of which is felt from time to time on the earth. Much as the radiation sent forth by the known planets around the earth affects both the individual and collective life of mankind, so also do these etheric planets influence men and their affairs; so that when catastrophes and cataclysms have occurred which are inexplicable in the ordinary terms of science, their cause may become understood when knowledge has been obtained concerning these powerful forces.

This raises the question whether or not men are merely puppets in the grip of mighty and unknown powers existent in an unseen and unrealised universe? This is a natural query of the physical mind or brain. But a mind no longer trammelled by its own materialism will realise that even a seeming catastrophe can prove to be a fundamental ordinance of an infinite Love outworking even to the last degree in the perfecting of God's wayward humanity. So wise a Mind, so comprehensive a Wisdom not only remembers and oversees the lives of individuals on the physical plane, but pervades the whole evolution of the human spirit (which is divine) through the whole gamut of experience. The powers of comprehension of the awakened human soul can only bow down before such magnificence and majesty to adore the Supreme Power, which has conceived so wonderful a Plan for the evolution of the whole of human life.

The effect of these unseen and unknown planets can be tremendously potent; but humanity as a whole can have a say in the direction of these forces, which indeed can bring on the one hand an uplifting and spiritualising effect into human life; and on the other forces which are destructive of all good. *It is the collective thought-life of men which decides all these issues.*

I AM endeavouring to touch on a subject so stupendous in its scope as to be almost beyond my power to clothe thought with words. I think I have been compelled to venture because of the many predictions sent to me during the latter years of my earth life regarding coming world-catastrophes and world-changes.

I would impress on all concerned that these changes will certainly come; that they are inevitable, because a new era is at hand when the cosmic Christ draws near to the earth. May His children recognise His power and His glory.

But it should always be realised that those who will reject Him are not wilfully mad, nor are they wicked, but are suffering from a lack of spiritual evolution. They will, therefore, be returned to a lower cycle of evolution and will thereafter journey onward by a different road from that taken by the souls which will prove ready to realise and welcome their Master.

Now to try to define what we mean by the cosmic Christ.

He is little understood today even by spiritually developed and intellectually advanced people, and there still lingers a pathetic confusion of thought concerning the divinity or deity of Jesus of Nazareth. The orthodox churches are guilty of almost as much materialism in their teaching as is Spiritualism, because they have seized on the physical aspect only of that wondrous presentation of the Infinite through the Initiate Jesus Christ, deifying the Nazarene himself and failing to recognise the infinite love and wisdom which manifested through him; failing to realise how tiny a conception is theirs of that mighty indwelling force—of that life ever more abundant known as the Son of God, the Son of the infinite and universal Being.

Throughout history many a prophet and seer came to prepare his way, to quicken humanity that it might receive so wondrous a manifestation of the Christ in the flesh. He came, he lived among men, and was despised and rejected by them.

There was a time when I also rejected the saving grace of Christ; and as I was led into Spiritualism I believe that it helped me to become a little less materialistic. Gradually I began to see the light and beauty revealed in the life of the Nazarene. At first, I accepted him as a wonderful prophet, seer and medium; as a noble brother and comrade to wayfaring man. Truly, he is the great brother of all humanity; but the quality of his brotherhood cannot be reconciled with any prevailing idea that he is merely a man much as ourselves. All is a question of degree; of the degree that Christ lives in us and we in him.

Let us always remember that even this manifestation through the body, soul and mind of Jesus was limited and partial; but surely it was enough to teach and to convince mankind that God is a God of love? By the example of his own life Jesus Christ demonstrated that the one way to eternal life and the Kingdom was through him; through man's identifying himself with his divine grace, his magnificent thought and tenderness, his transcendent love and mercy, which is the one saving grace for poor humanity.

This truth will be very clearly demonstrated within the next few years.★ Man can already see its signs and portents creeping on his world; see the undermining of the rotten systems which are ruled by self, the bitter fruits of wars which are past and wars which are to come, of armaments, reparations and tariffs. It is to be demonstrated to a sad and bewildered world that some day all people must bow down to the one Power which alone can save humanity from utter destruction—even the saving power and grace of Christ as demonstrated through Jesus of Nazareth.

II

WE have touched on many vital points, and our task is now to enlarge on these, to fill the vacant places and paint a fuller picture. We have already spoken about the cosmic spheres and have left the soul in that condition. We have suggested that it is from the cosmic spheres that the Great Ones are sent forth on their mission to mankind. We would add that when the average man arrives at long last at this stage of his evolution and has reached the cosmic spheres, he has finished with physical life, for it is no longer necessary for him to return; but as regards his finer spiritual consciousness there are still great heights to scale. These cannot be attained without even further experience of living, but not now on the earth. We therefore direct your attention to the planets to which we have alluded; those planets

---

★ When these words were spoken Europe had already travelled far along that *karmic* path which ensured the suffering which was to come with the Second Great War. Few realised it, however.

of ethereal substance or 'matter', which were they of denser etheric substance might radiate a light which would sometimes be visible to the astronomer.

There are many souls who, having finished their 'course' on earth, advance in communities or groups to recommence existence on one or other of these more highly evolved planets. To do so they descend through various spheres which envelop these planets—spheres which correspond in a sense to the astral, mental and celestial spheres which surround the earth—although they are of finer quality, greater radiance, because of their higher and more spiritual vibrancy.

These communities of spirits descend by easy stages and ultimately manifest in what might be called physical bodies; but I can never describe the beauty of their forms. Suffice it to say that all these conditions of life are wonderful indeed, because here all the laws of spiritual life are working out harmoniously to their destined end. Life in such a form as this is without limitations as men are aware of limitations, not only on their earth but on the higher astral planes which surround it; for such a life becomes veritably illimitable. Who can conceive even a tithe of the pervading glory and fullness to which man can attain, the ultimate grandeur of his destiny and being? Yet even advanced beings such as these cannot forget what bondage in matter must mean to men, and are compassionate; this is why, when humanity is in dire straits, communities of the angelic ones direct the light of their compassion earthward.

There are even souls who descend from the celestial spheres to become spiritual guides, being reborn on the astral plane instead of the physical. They undertake this work at their own choice, and at considerable sacrifice. They can and do, of course, gain much new experience through the intimate contact with humanity which the work of a guide entails.

We have already spoken about reincarnation. You are told by some people that this is true, by others that it is false. Both are right from their own particular viewpoint; there are so many, many forms of life waiting for man to experience—forms too numerous for him to comprehend—so that while souls do continually return to earth to incarnate again, many refrain. This may sound somewhat contradictory, in view of what has been said in a previous communication. In our condition, however, no soul is ever forced to adopt or follow one particular path of progression or form of living; although eventually it must conform to all the laws of the spiritual life because it is itself essentially spirit. To help you to understand this I give a crude illustration. Try to imagine millions of atoms seething in an etheric surround; then observe that each atom is reacting to an attractive power in accordance with its own particular quality or essence. Each atom must incline towards that power, as if drawn by a magnet, following its own path of evolution. This is why when the ego—which means the divine spark resident in man—is projected from the Creative Intelligence which man calls God, to live in *form* out in the world, it must still feel the 'tug' of one or other of those myriad spirals of evolution which are ever open to the evolving soul.

While all souls have eventually to conform to the law, and work out their destiny in accordance with the law, each soul stays absolutely *individual*. Does not this give you some insight into the depth of meaning within those words of the Master Jesus when he said, 'Even the hairs of your head are numbered'? From the waster in the gutter to the wisest man in your land, in its degree every soul remains attuned to Divine Intelligence, and therefore must ultimately follow the particular pathway which will lead it back to God.

CHAPTER VIII

THE ENNOBLEMENT OF LIFE BOTH
INCARNATE AND DISCARNATE

'In this land the Shining Ones commonly walked, because it was upon the borders of heaven . . . And this the Gardener said, even to me.'

—John Bunyan.

I

WE have now (and you must help us) to connect the various faiths or religions of humanity with the spheres of astral, mental and celestial life from which they derive their power. For, when man grasps that he lives and creates not only in the 'here and now' of his daily life, but also in that life beyond wherein he will enter into a fuller recognition of himself, he will begin to alter his outlook. This new understanding of his real nature will raise his ideals, ennoble his actions, and inspire him with finer ambitions than those which might leave him enmeshed after his death on the lower planes of the astral life; for he will assuredly find himself bound to these, if he be not raised out of his lower self.

If you will study and compare the religions of past and present all will be found to spring from one common source or fount, which is the Universal. It does not matter whether they be ancient or modern—the ancient Egyptian, the Chaldean, the Greek, the wisdom of the Hindu, or the various orthodox Christian Churches of our day, or Christian Science, or Theosophy, and indeed the higher Spiritualism All will be found to possess one common element within—the universal sphere or cosmic consciousness. From this Centre springs that ultimate ideal of a life of perfect harmony for man which inspires all religion, together with the promise of a life redeemed wherein the soaring and sinless soul is merged into one illimitable sea of peace and bliss. From that one Centre all religion, while it remains pure and undefiled, draws its sustenance. . . .

How I wish that I could make the links for you with this Centre . . . if I can only make it all clear! I will try; but if I fail you must use your own faculties to help me. Try. Ask me a question.

Question: *We do not follow you. What does the phrase ' make a link' mean?*

Let me illustrate. In Christian Science there exists a very definite link with the mental plane on the part of those calling themselves Christian Scientists. Through exercise of their mental body, and through their intellect (for this is partly a religion of the intellect) the Scientists are certainly in contact with the first mental plane, that of hard intellectual thought or realisation. What I am trying to show is that every religion is attached to one or other of the various planes of the spiritual life we are describing. The Spiritualists are in the main only in contact with beings or entities from the astral planes; for this reason Spiritualism as a religion is largely confined to these seven astral planes. The pure and ancient religion known as Buddhism was originally linked to the third heavenly or celestial sphere, the ultimate aspiration of the devout Buddhist being to reach ' nirvana' or the plane of meditation from which the soul emerges into the universal. This has been erroneously deemed a condition of ' nothingness'. What we have to realise is that the ultimate goal of all men is to attain to a condition of God-awareness or God-consciousness; where the personality dwindles and is absorbed, and the human individuality becomes so *at one* with the Universal that in surrendering itself it becomes a very pulse in the mighty Being of God. Then indeed does self relinquish self. Such is the ultimate, the highest to which we can point.

Even this does not mean that the individual man will become so absorbed in God that he cannot afterwards, by exercise of his will and intelligence, be detached from the Whole to manifest as a separate intelligence again. We realise that the average man shrinks from the thought of absorption because he has immersed himself in his own development as a personality. Yet every soul will eventually have to be ready to let itself go and so to become a part of the one universal Life Force, because only when it reaches this stage does it become greater than itself. This is the point at which 'the Father and I are one' as Jesus said . . . We have already discussed this subject.

Question: *What of the faith of ancient Egypt?*

The truths which we are trying to transmit can be found in the religion of ancient Egypt. What we have to say contains no more than a restatement of its store of wisdom and truth.

Question: *What about modern religions such as Theosophy?*

We would reply that the Theosophy of the ancients contained in its essence these vital truths, but Theosophy today, like many another religion and system of belief, has become distorted, with its original foundation broken or split, so that there are many differing ideas difficult to unify. The pure Theosophy which sprang from the Ancient Wisdom finds embodiment in our teaching. The branch known as Theosophy today is mainly linked to the first mental plane.

Question: *What about the Protestant Church?*

This is a religion based on a wonderful and pure teaching; but it has become overridden by creed and dogma. It is my work to try to unify, to create harmony and never to destroy, so you will understand that I have to choose my words, and give carefully thought-out answers to your questions. Therefore I prefer not to separate the various branches of the Christian religion into denominations but to take it as a whole, and relate it to the life of the spirit as I find it in these realms of the discarnate.

If you study the teachings of the Master Jesus you will find that from beginning to end they embody truth, simplicity and a vast depth of understanding of human need, together with a creative power and wisdom which can open the door of heaven to every human soul who wills to enter by the path of love and brotherhood. They contain truths which will bring a follower of Christ to a life of perfect health, harmony and happiness. They embody a religion which if faithfully followed and lived, will link the human soul to every sphere, astral and mental, and to the ultimate Universal.

We have spoken about a sphere of *conscious* reunion—the only words we can find—wherein all the kingdoms of life, the vegetable and animal, the human, the spirit realm, the angelic and the divine, can meet as one. When thus inspired the soul of man is responsive to and recognises its friendship and kinship with every beast and flower. It is here that men known as Masters, who have attained mastership over the lower forms of life by strict training and endeavour, can hold in their will, in their intelligence, the lesser will and desire of their brothers and sisters of lowlier forms of existence.

This may be a subject difficult for you to grasp. We refer to a condition of mastery which all men will some day share. Stories in your Bible and in the Scriptures of other races tell of wild beasts and men meeting with common understanding and respect one for the other. I mention two instances, but many another could be quoted. I speak of Daniel in the lions' den, and of Balaam's ass, two apparent fables, yet which present a profound awareness of that sphere of conscious reunion of which we speak, where all creatures attain to the recognition of universal kinship. The episode of the unbroken colt which Jesus rode into Jerusalem will at once occur. Do you not see whither this new understanding of our true nature is leading us, the great potentialities it contains, the new humanity it may awaken?

You will presently realise with some surprise that as we proceed we are completing a structure which is now only in process of formation in the course of these homely talks. Again and again we would emphasise the one recurring theme—that we are living in ' our life after death ' *here and now*. This is what we have to bring home once and for all; not merely to prove to man that he survives death, but to show him that behind all life the universal and creative power of God ever labours; and further, to prove to him that until he realises its might and potency, and thereafter inclines his heart to living in brotherhood with all creatures, he himself will never find lasting peace of heart, happiness or harmony.

Brotherhood must always come first; and then will follow a new freedom gained through contact with heaven during man's life on earth. . . . That is it . . . Brotherhood, the Great White Brotherhood, on earth as it is in heaven—that is the ideal.

II

I have been considering the notes of our last talk. You will wonder how this is done. I was very pleased to see Minesta studying the notes herself, because through her mind I was able to get a fairly clear idea of what had been recorded, and felt tempted to insert and correct as I should have done in the old days. I see that one or two points need elucidation. First let me amplify my statement that Spiritualism is in the main related to the astral spheres. On consideration the reason becomes obvious; Spiritualists as a whole desire a personal contact with their friends in spirit, and this contact is mostly with the astral world. Pursuit of this desire becomes a science for the psychic researcher, a religion for the bereaved and lonely soul.

During the many years I spent in spreading the gospel of Spiritualism my dominant thought was to bring comfort to the bereaved. As a man filled with warm human love for my fellow creatures, having a family which I adored, I sympathised intensely with those left lonely. My dominant thought was to give assurance to those poor folk that those whom they had loved and lost were neither dead nor far away, but so close that they could commune with them, and that they were living on in a condition of peace and joy. Don't you understand that to me at that time this seemed so urgent and vital a realisation that all else in comparison faded into insignificance?

It is true; man possesses within himself the power to create his own after-death conditions; which are affected by his visions, his ideas of God, and of the after-life and of heaven. As his imagination quickens, so he forms an ideal according to his capacity. Barbaric man sets up graven images of his God for worship, the best and highest he can conceive. So also with the average man or woman of today; each formulates an idea or ideal of God and of the next life, according to his or her depth of thought and feeling. Thus the man who concentrates on human love and family ties, on personal contacts and physical comforts, engenders within himself a commensurate idea of heaven. So also did I conceive my idea of heaven and felt that all folk who loved each other as we ourselves loved *and love still*, must feel exactly as I then felt; that all people must dread and shrink from the idea of inevitable parting even as we ourselves once dreaded it until we had established faith in survival based on evidence and truth.

So the average enquirer into Spiritualism is moved by this one reason—to make contact, personal contact, with someone he loves in spirit. Can you think of anything more joyful, more comforting than to find that soul again, to know that a lost father, mother, husband, wife, brother, sister, or child, can still commune across the gulf? It is true, very wonderfully true! Those who pass on linger, as we have told you, in the astral planes of life, so necessarily it must be true that Spiritualism derives its origin from the astral. Rarely do beings from the celestial regions return unless they have a definite mission to perform.

The astral planes are not planes of accomplishment. For this reason Spiritualism lacks the power which attracts and holds those of other faiths. We, by means of this fresh influx of knowledge, hope to restore this power. We are endeavouring to link the movement to the spheres of power. For the attracting force, the love which endures, and the wisdom which kindles the life and fire of religion always comes from the celestial spheres, not from the astral.

We Spiritualists have much to learn. We too must fling wide our doors, so that Wisdom, Power and Love may enter in to abide with us. Not for one moment, however, would I decry Spiritualists because they contact chiefly the astral planes. God knows I would be the last to do so, because I have seen and known the wonderful consolation and the joy which comes to people on *both* sides of the grave by means of spirit communion. But one might almost segregate communications into two separate grades: communication which is but experimental; and communion of the spirit, which will some day grow so pure and blessed as to become sacramental. Communion such as this must come as a holy and blessed form of dedication, meant for the ennoblement of life both incarnate and discarnate. It is true that time, new education and realisations are necessary to dispel the present-day ignorance of these matters. May this work of ours serve that purpose, at least to a degree, by bringing a gleam of God's truth to men!

The other branch of investigation, that of psychical research, should have its doors rigidly shut against the curious and the sensation-seeker. There should no longer be exploitation of the sensitive human instruments through which contact with the beyond comes. All must be put into proper place; law and order must come in these matters, and a more reverent understanding of the beauty and wonder of mediumship.

Let us realise that the rituals of the Roman Catholic and High Anglican Churches are designed to call on the planes of power. One can at once feel this potency on entering any church where high ritual is practised. Everything—the incense, the way the censer is used, and even the form of administration of the blessing —is practised with deliberate intention to create this power and distribute it among the worshippers. I have visited many a church since I became discarnate to witness this process at work. I have seen how the strains of music influence the minds of the worshippers; how they themselves contribute to the power by the action of their emotional body. On the other hand, in nonconformist churches, where ornate ritual has become a plain and simple devotion, if a true purity of heart and purpose be present a power will also gather, but of a somewhat different order. In some of these, however, a spiritual coldness creeps in, a lack of fire and life due to complacency, so that those who gather to worship tend to become over-satisfied with themselves, to think themselves God's chosen people. (I shall be severely criticised, but this also has been noted in my journeyings.)

As to the wisdom and rightness of using ritual, music, and the like, to attract and to maintain power over the people, we remind you that there can be use and abuse of all things. Doubtless power rightly obtained and rightly put to use forms part of the creative plan, since such powers lie within man waiting for use; and if by knowledge and intelligence and by purity of ideals and aspirations the man becomes linked to the higher celestial spheres, he attracts these powers to himself by his own spiritual growth.

We have told you that the Christian religion was the purest, containing as it does a kernel of pure truth. We would now elucidate this statement: we shall be challenged as to the doctrine of the vicarious atonement and the meaning of the words, ' *I am the way, the truth and the life. No man cometh to the Father but by Me.*' This is still a sad stumbling block to many people. They have yet to realise, as I now realise, the spiritual meaning behind these words.

We do not propound any gospel of vicarious atonement. We are assured that as a man sows so must he surely reap: that nobody else can ever take from him the responsibility of his own evil thinking and doing. But when a man, however sunken, reaches that point where his soul is illumined by a truth created by and through the power and the love of Christ, he is born again and his old self dies. In that way only does Christ preserve him, redeem him from ignorance, sin and darkness, and point him to eternal life. To every soul, whether Spiritualist, Orthodox Christian, Buddhist, Atheist, there will come this dawning of the light of God; or, in other words, this coming of Christ the Beloved; for every soul, no matter what its label, however much it deny its Master, must some day enter heaven through the ' narrow gate ', through the immeasurable love and the perfect wisdom of the compassionate Christ.

On the last occasion we spoke of the Buddhist belief. This too needs amplification. The Buddhist of today holds that the ultimate and supreme goal of his existence is to enter the sphere of life known to him as nirvana. He therefore desires to reincarnate as speedily as possible in order that he may hasten through many a life and ultimately reach freedom from rebirth. He believes that nirvana will release him from this eternal round. In nirvana he will find peace, having lost himself in desirelessness, in nothingness. His error lies in his interpretation of the teachings of the Buddha. So also are the teachings of Jesus presented in very different guise from the truths given to his disciples two thousand years ago.

The Lord Buddha came to point the way to that ultimate surrender which every human soul must make, which is the resignation of itself to the Supreme. By his own profound experience he had proved that only as a little child in simplicity and trust can a man enter the kingdom. This he taught his people.

One more point; if you follow the true vision of the spirit, you will find all this truth in the ancient wisdom—the source of all religion both of the East and West. You will find the place of the disquieted spirits described, the higher astral spheres, the mental, celestial and universal spheres of life. All the teachers through all the ages have returned to earth with much the same revelation. What a glorious destiny is thus revealed to any man ready to renounce self and its desires for the service of man and God.

CHAPTER IX

THE HEALING OF ALL DISEASE

IT is truly said that medical science will be compelled some day to study pyschic and spiritual laws.* When I recall the operations I once had to witness as a doctor, I now shudder with horror and disgust. Yet I appreciate the fact that many lives are being saved by the skill of the surgeon. But I dare to add that many more lives (and the sanity thereof) will be saved when the medical world makes a study of man's astral body and its well-being.

Certain rays exist which, when men can open themselves to the Divine Intelligence, can be used to heal their bodies. This will depend not so much on the quality of the healer's intellect as on his spiritual intelligence or insight, which will enable him to attract these rays to himself (much as a magnet attracts), and redirect the light through his patient. This is only one of the new ways of healing some day to be assimilated when Medicine is open to receive information concerning light and colour rays.

How truly has it been said that all that is needed for health, healing and sustenance waits in the Universal for man's use and comfort. Unfortunately, however, those who are spiritually ignorant cannot draw on this abundance of God's supply.

It is equally difficult, if not impossible, for those who possess

---

* It will be seen that A.C.D. assumes that his reader both understands and accepts the existence and reality of the etheric and astral bodies as part of earthly man; and furthermore that some day the medical world will accept this truth, and find its outlook, and treatment of disease, revolutionised because of it; realising that disease of the body is something at its final stage of externalisation after a long period of inner causation. In other words, some day medicine will study the *causes*, where it is at present trying to cure the *effects* of disease. It is from this standpoint that A.C.D. begins his message on the cause and cure of all disease.

this knowledge to convey it to others. It must dawn from the soul's own understanding; and the time will surely come when Light from the Cosmic Christ will thus illumine man's enshadowed understanding. He will then awaken out of darkness.

I AM not working singly in this matter: I am but one of a band of workers and have been purposely strengthened and taught many things. It has been my particular task to be the spokesman, and so bring these messages back. Much that I pass on has been given to me for that special purpose, although my mind has caught many a glimpse of the glories I attempt to describe. I know that these things *are*, but cannot truly say that I have experienced all these wonders; and yet . . . it would seem at times as though the whole panorama of human life opens before me, and I see not only into the past but into the future of the world and of humanity. Great changes are coming; a wonderful light is streaming down on to the earth, and humanity is responding. According to the degree of its response, so will humanity become more spiritual and its world more etherealised.

Maybe, my friends, you would like us to speak of something more akin to your own human life, more simple, more understandable to you. *Dear friends, these things of which we speak are among the simplest of God's gifts to His children.*

DURING past centuries many methods of healing sickness have become known and practised. Each would appear to be effective, but only in certain cases, and none in all. It is now our task to trace the source of the healer's power, as well as seek out the origin of disease. In spite of the controversy these statements may arouse, disease originates, not as may be thought in the mental state of the patient, but usually far deeper. It may sometimes begin in man's conscious mind, it is true, sometimes in the subconscious, but more often in the *pre-conscious*. By the last term we mean a condition of consciousness far older than the life now being lived, but one which can be brought over from the man's past lives; a consciousness which extends back through many 'ages' or incarnations. But this must not be confused with what is known to the psychologist as man's 'racial instinct.'

We suggest that the pre-conscious mind appertains to man's ego, to his spirit, whereas what might be called his instinctive mind appertains to the animal and racial instincts which may be inherent; but are not necessarily related to or co-ordinated with the pre-consciousness of man, which is a part of the universal or spiritual heritage which all men share. It would seem that this pre-conscious state is unknown in the animal world.

The public today is more concerned with man's conscious and subconscious minds, recognising that they are responsible for many of the minor complaints of the body and can even aggravate some of its major complaints. There are also many diseases the cause of which cannot be traced to the conscious or subconscious minds.

We have mentioned the healers' source of supply, but have yet to classify the healers into their several sections. We now do so as follows:

Magnetic or Psychic Healers;
Mental Healers such as the Christian Scientists;
Hypnotic Healers;
Dietist or Nature Healers;
Spiritual Healers;
Sacramental Healers;
Manipulative Healers such as the Osteopaths;
Occult Healers;
Colour-Ray Healers.

Each of these can bring about cures in some cases, but none in all. It should be made clear that each type, when treating pain and disease, treats not only the physical but also the etheric and mental bodies of the patient. We repeat that all major diseases result from lack of harmony between man's psychic and physical bodies, and that the physical is the last to manifest the illness. In all the varieties of healing set forth the healer must discover some point of contact with his patient, otherwise he cannot bring about a cure. Thus, it is obvious that no one healer can cure every case. We would also suggest that herbal remedies should not be forgotten, because many cases can be more effectively treated in this manner than by pouring out psychic power on a localised infection. It is true, but not generally realised, that certain herbs and drugs act not only on the physical but also on the etheric body of man, which is very similar but of much looser texture. Some of these drugs cause the etheric body to loosen its grip on poisons and congestions which are the outcome of the patient's conscious, subconscious or pre-conscious disharmony in the mental body.

Here, it is as well to emphasise that the term 'mental body' does not necessarily apply to the physico-mental body—the outer mentality of man which is directly related to the brain. For there is an astral-mental body directly related to the desire or emotional nature; and a third mental body to the celestial or universal mind. I hope that this does not confuse the issue, but will help you to realise that as the conscious mind, by thinking erroneously, can so influence and weaken the cell-consciousness of the physical body as to create disease, so also can the universal or pre-conscious mind control and purify the cell-consciousness by operating through man's higher mind, and thus cure all disease by a process of elimination. And that is why we say that there is no disease on the earth-plane which is incurable.

We declare that all human life is divided into rays of varying vibrations, and that it is ruled by such rays. We will describe only twelve of these rays, and be content with that.

Shall we say that all humanity vibrates to one or other of these twelve rays or vibrations? Therefore, if a healer attempts to treat a man vibrating on, say, a number seven ray with a number five method of treatment he will certainly fail, and may do more harm than good. If, however, he treats his number seven patient with treatment suitable for number seven, he will effect a cure.

Vibrations are expressed in colour; that is to say, colour is the outward and visible symbol of vibration. We will try to enumerate the colours corresponding to their respective numbers as follows:— First, the Red ray; second, the Green; third, Blue; fourth, Pink; fifth, Yellow; sixth, Purple; seventh, Violet; eighth, Lavender; ninth, Pearl; tenth, Silver; eleventh, Golden; and twelfth, pure White.

It will be the first task of the colour healer to discover the colour of the ray on which his patient vibrates. In accordance with the colour and number of his ray, so will the patient be liable to certain weaknesses, and will need either a sedative or stimulating ray to balance and restore harmony in his being.

It will be found that the yellow ray is a particularly fine colour for treating tuberculosis; that the blue ray gives the best results in nervous diseases; that the red ray is useful for all poisonous conditions of the blood; and that the violet and the green rays are both curative of cancer.

With certain patients the psychic centres to be treated will vary (we are aware that we have not yet specified them and in due course shall do so). In some cases the throat is the most sensitive and therefore receptive spot on which to direct the green ray. With others the heart will give a powerful response to the violet ray, and will also prove an efficacious centre through which to treat blood diseases or blood poisoning; for the violet light cleanses and purifies the bloodstream as it flows to and from the heart.

WE repeat that we cannot claim that this light-ray treatment will prove effective for every person. We have given the table of colours and their corresponding numbers. We are trying to suggest rather than dogmatise.

A prevalent cause of disease is the sufferer's inability to relax. Most of you, unconsciously or consciously, live taut and tense, in both your waking and your sleeping hours. When you fall asleep with a tense mind, unconsciously your finger, elbow and knee joints, the spinal column and all such bony parts, retain a corresponding tensity. This is often because much the same condition prevails during the daily life. The tension of the body is due to a mental condition of fear, worry, suppressed emotion or suppressed desire. Hence during sleeping or waking a hold-up occurs at the various centres of the sufferer's psychic bodies.

If people would learn from childhood the importance of relaxation by making it a habit, thus going through daily life restfully, in harmony with themselves, with others and with God, they would retain that vital and perfect rhythmic flow round and through their psychic and physical bodies. This flow by its very nature carries away all waste matter, which is cast off or eliminated, and caught up by the universal to be absorbed and transformed into fresh power. When breathing out you exhale poison. For exhaling is the continual casting away of outworn physical and psychical matter. Conversely, inhaling should be an indrawing of the pure *prana*, the universal life-force which can sustain the body in rhythmic and perfect health.

It is therefore misleading to state, as does the Christian Scientist, that all disease originates in what Christian Science calls ' the mortal mind '. Disease lies deeper. Nevertheless, as soon as a person can relax his mortal mind, and reach out to draw on the fresh and universal life force, he automatically sets an inflow in motion which will in time create a perfect body.

DOES the cause of an accident lie hidden in the pre-conscious mind of its victim; or is the person merely the victim of some cruel mischance? Even accidents are the result of inharmony previously created deep within the pre-conscious self. This may seem a hard doctrine, but on examination is not so; any soul falling victim to accident knows well in its pre-consciousness that it has a lesson only to be learned by undergoing such an experience.

Soon somebody will be asking us about children; about poor little sufferers who have been born as the result of drunken lust, or from diseased parents. Are we to conclude that these innocents have been doomed by fate to undergo a life of suffering?

What about souls that are imprisoned in the body of a lunatic, or in bodies corrupt with disease from birth? How can questions such as these find any rational answer?

We reply that the same law applies: the soul of man always possesses foreknowledge of what is to happen, and power to accept or reject the kind of life which is offered to it. It is impossible for man with his very limited insight into these deeper matters to grasp the motive which induced a soul to accept and undergo a life of suffering, or even to glimpse the degree of suffering that soul is undergoing. Still more must he refrain from judging that omnipotent Power which man, even when appalled by some horror he has seen, still tries to call good, God, the first great Cause; that Cause which must see little children suffer and apparently heed them not!

Over here we do not judge anyone; with broader vision we do not see a God vindictive or cruel in any aspect; but we are always aware of an infinite Love, a divine and compassionate Intelligence, ever merciful to man. We see an All-wise Fatherhood ever giving His children power of freewill to choose their path; a path which either by suffering or by joy, by conquest over egoism and selfhood, ever wends its way upward and back into the supreme consciousness of the Cosmos wherein perfection dwells.

A sentimentalist watching a cat playing with a mouse shudders, exclaiming, ' How awful, how cruel a thing is this! Nature seems full of cruelty.' So it may appear, but only to someone with limited vision It is not so; behind all outer semblance the love and the understanding of God permeate all things. The suffering so apparent around us cloaks a method of bringing realisation of God's supreme harmony, love and beauty into the consciousness of God's creatures—yes, even the least of them.

WE have touched on the effect of the *pre-conscious* mind in its relation to disease, in the hope that it will help you to understand why apparently good and even saintly people can contract painful and even mortal complaints. In face of these happenings, it seems of little avail to protest, to question the apparent injustice of such happenings. The cause lies far deeper than the sweet and gentle nature of the person concerned. It reaches back far beyond the sufferer's present span of life or incarnation, and its roots cannot be found in the here and now of the outer life. Like a fever, the suffering heralds a cleaning up, a clearing out, an end of a process. An agnostic may regard such suffering much as our sentimentalist regards the mouse caught by a cat, seeing only days and nights of pain; and reckoning nothing of the root and blossoms which the sufferer's tree of life will eventually bear as the result. Accordingly he remains ignorant of that germ of a life-more-abundant which stirs within, and which will spring forth bright and beautiful from the soil thus ploughed and harrowed. He sees, he knows, only the surface of man's being. The true life of the soul is hidden from him.

It is of interest to know that the outer and subversive emotions of anger, greed and jealousy can create the simpler diseases, distinct from those which are deeply rooted in the soul. Self-pity, for instance, can and frequently does induce back-ache and kidney trouble. It can also affect the liver, although any violent emotions can cause trouble in that quarter; as a result poison is driven into the blood stream. Fear and worry, if prolonged, can do much the same sort of thing and may even eventuate in cancer. If one could perceive the origin of a sufficient number of cancer cases it would be found that deep-rooted fear had induced a state of tensity, thereby closing in the etheric body, and causing a hold-up of the psychic flow already described.

It has been said that the outer emotions can cause definite disease. It must always be remembered, however, that man does not give rein to these harmful emotions unless his mind is uncontrolled. This brings us back to the fact that inner harmony is all important so far as health is concerned; and a state of inner harmony is dependent on the arising of man's spiritual self.

Does his diet affect the wellbeing of man? Yes, in some cases quickly, in others after long delay. Some will not be affected at all. The man who has reached a condition of peace of mind and lives harmoniously by reason of his understanding of divine laws could not abuse his body by over-eating or the wrong choice of food. Indigestion is brought about mostly by the conscious mind of the patient.

It is of great interest to us to see from this side the source of the inspiration of some of our prominent writers. I am reminded of the play, *The Blue Bird*, by Maeterlinck. In one scene the children are assembled awaiting their call to return to earth; each carries a bag containing not only the gifts and accomplishments the child will bring back, but also the complaints he will suffer from, such as whooping cough, scarlet fever and so forth, all neatly packed for them before they sail in Father Time's ship across the starry seas to their waiting mothers on earth!

A fairy story, some will say; but nevertheless a tremendous truth is here unfolded, which may have filtered down from the Universal or arisen from some pre-conscious level of the writer's own self.

THE psychic healer can accomplish valuable work in that he can relieve the congestion of the psychic bodies. There are some whom he cannot help because he cannot probe deeply enough into the patient's real trouble. He can help best when the patient will help himself. In this sort of psychic-spiritual healing it will be noticed that when the disease has been apparently cured, or when the patient's ' house ' has been swept and garnished, if that patient lapse from contact with the higher forces again, his condition of health may be even worse than before. The parable of the man who was dispossessed of the devil, whose house was swept and garnished, but left empty, so that on his return he found it possessed by seven other devils including the old one, well illustrates our meaning.

We repeat, it is futile for any one kind of healer to claim to be able to heal every disease. We have touched on the twelve rays, and in this connection would direct your minds to the twelve ' signs ' of the zodiac, to the twelve ' tribes ' of Israel, to the mystery and significance of this number ' twelve,' suggesting that here is a reference to the twelve rays under which the human family can be grouped. Every herb comes under one or other of these twelve rays. The sage of old discovered that for every disease a corresponding herb could be gathered, which vibrated to the same number and colour and would produce a magical effect. The origin of many an ancient custom, many a magical potion, can be traced back to this knowledge.

The numbers four and three are powerful numbers so far as the human family is concerned and affect man in all his affairs. *The basis of the world's calculation* was set on the symbols of the square and the triangle in the dim past. Ponder the significance of the great Pyramid of Egypt, standing as it does as a mathematical symbol of life itself!

Now the twelve ' houses ' or ' tribes ', or the twelve rays on which the human family vibrates, must again be divided into four. These four are indeed Earth, Air, Fire and Water. Some day, when the physician of a distant future desires to treat a patient, he will first cast that patient's horoscope. This is not a fantastic notion; we are in earnest. We are trying to give a chart or ruling by which man may some day, if he cares to, discover the cause of every disease. He will do this by casting the patient's horoscope—not the usual kind of horoscope, but the kind which reaches out beyond this particular life to the whole being of the ego and reveals the rays on which it has vibrated during its many incarnations. It will be found by this method that all disease can be classified into one or other of the four groups; and when it appears that the patient vibrates to the Earth sign, or that of Water, or Fire or Air, an appropriate remedy will be found under that sign in place of the one remedy now being given to all and sundry. It will also be learned that people vibrating under one or other of these signs become prone to certain diseases and can be safeguarded against them.

HAVING touched on the twelve rays of vibration, it is now our task to speak of the twelve points of their contact. Starting from the heart as a central point, we shall number them thus:

1. The heart;
2. The throat;
3. The pineal gland;
4. The pituitary gland;
5. The spleen;
6. The base of the spine;
7. The solar plexus;
8. The organs of generation;
9 & 10. The two hands;
11 & 12. The two feet.

It can and will be proved some day by an instrument that these twelve psychic centres are very susceptible to the rays of healing. It is true that the human body and the quickening spirit within that body should be able to cure itself without outside aid; moreover, it can attract and pass on rays which should heal other people. We have already explained, however, that some complaints are so superficial and trivial that they can be readily dealt with by surface application. It seems simpler to treat a boil by fomentations rather than by magnetic or spiritual healing.

It will also be found that a corresponding organ of the body is linked to each of the psychic centres. For instance, by treating the throat centre with a certain colour-ray—which is but a vibration, you understand—a reaction will follow not so much in the throat as in the stomach.

The pituitary gland must be the centre treated in cases of obsession and mental derangement. Epilepsy has long baffled medical science. It may not surprise you to hear that this disease originates because of a maladjustment of the psychic bodies caused by some spiritual or psychic disharmony of the parents when the child was conceived. I wonder whether we have any conception of the responsibilities of parenthood? It has been said that the sins of the fathers shall be visited on the children even unto the third and fourth generation. Even so, the saying has a deeper meaning, and might be more truly interpreted as ' the sins of the man shall revisit him even unto the third and fourth *incarnation.*' Surely our earlier incarnations are the ' father ' to those which follow on?

The question of how epilepsy is to be cured will arise. Must it ever remain one of those obscure diseases that afflict the whole life-period of a sufferer? Epilepsy is only curable if a re-adjustment of the psychic bodies of the patient can be brought about by making a connecting link between the pituitary and the pineal glands. When this gap opens the epileptic fit occurs. To put it more plainly, we suggest that there is ' a screw loose.' When the apparatus slips, at that moment the fit occurs. Tighten up the screw, or get a perfect alignment of the psychic bodies, and you cure the case.

WE would like to group diseases under their respective signs of Earth, Air, Fire and Water, and suggest appropriate treatment, bearing in mind that we must also consider the three sections within each sign, namely the mineral, animal and vegetable. Let us take first:—

The Air Sign: Those under this group will often suffer from nervous diseases which act through the psychic centres. The head and back will be the most frequently affected. Usually the psychic centre which responds best will be the base of the spine.

The Fire Sign: Here patients will be emotional, likely to suffer from obsession or mental troubles, inflammations and fevers. Treatment in all such cases should be by the pituitary and pineal glands.

The Earth Sign: The phlegmatic, the type liable to accumulate poison because of general sluggishness and lack of that flow of which I spoke, can be grouped under this heading. There will be catarrhal conditions and subsequent poisons in the blood, and other diseases which originate from such causes.

The Water Sign: Strange as it may seem the Water sign affects the lower part of the body, the legs and feet. This being a fluidic sign, those under it can be best helped by psychic or magnetic treatment. Those under the fiery sign respond readily to colour-ray treatment; those under the airy sign to spiritual and sacramental treatment; and those under the earthy sign to dietetic and mental treatment such as that of Christian Science, and methods of a similar character.

If people would only follow out these hints—and mark, they are no more than hints—if they would use but a fraction of the application, experiment and research that is poured out without stint on an inexact and speculative medical science, an exact and scientific method of universal healing would come about, based on a real knowledge of man's physical, psychic and spiritual nature. If man really wishes, healing can become certain and precise in method.

WE have mentioned treatment by herbal remedies. Herbs are available which correspond in vibration and colour to each of the twelve sections, and suitable herbs can be selected to treat those under the fire, the water, the earth or air signs; the right herb will prove beneficial in every case, whereas the wrong one might be harmful.

Herbs grow under very definite laws; their growth is not wholly due to climate or season, but takes form and character from certain rays which rule life on earth in the mineral, vegetable and animal kingdoms. That is why the healer should have knowledge of his patient's astrological make-up, for every medicinal herb can be classified by its own sign of the zodiac. A herb should be selected which accords with the nature of the disease and of the patient. For instance, someone who is grouped under the rising sign of Leo should be prescribed a herb of that number and ray, and forbidden one under a foreign ray. Accordingly it should be possible to classify and catalogue herbal remedies with considerable exactitude and precision.

Herbal treatment does not fulfil every requirement of healing. The patient should also be treated by his healer according to his sign and particular temperament. Asthma is a complaint caused through the nervous system, and such a form of nervous reaction or broken rhythm can be efficaciously treated by colour, using the blue or green ray. We believe that asthma falls into line with other nervous diseases and has a psychic origin. Sometimes magnetic treatment will cure. The centre to treat is the solar plexus. As there may be digestive derangement care should be given to the diet.

Many an attack of asthma is brought on by indiscretions of this sort, while worry or mental trouble will frequently herald its appearance. Remove the mental cause and the asthma disappears. Hence you will readily see why the blue ray, the calming, peace-restoring ray, is necessary here. To *breathe* or inhale certain drugs is merely to treat the *symptom*. Go to the root cause, which is psychic derangement, which usually centres around the solar plexus. Children who suffer from this complaint usually inherit it from the overwrought nervous system of the mother. This statement will doubtless be rejected; but it is nevertheless true, although there is the consoling thought that the complaint never recurs when once the soul has undergone this particular form of purification.

Cancer comes under the earth sign in some cases but not always; for it occasionally originates in the breaking of a very sacred law in some previous incarnation, and can be one of the methods chosen by its victim to erase that particular sin.

Medical science will some day discover that a cure for cancer lies in the treatment of the etheric body. Treatment will consist in the persistent action on the etheric body of a specified drug or herb. We mention ' gentian ' as one of the most powerful. Light-ray treatment is also of value, the pearl ray being one of the most efficacious cleansing rays for the etheric body. When the etheric matter composing the latter becomes relaxed and loosened by the action of the herb or the light-ray, there should follow a dispersal of the seat of the cancer in the physical body. Although cancer shows itself in one particular part, it is not always localised. Often an operation proves only an irritant to the disease, which chases through the blood stream and forms another little township.

LET me answer another question which can be stated thus: If diseases are brought over from a pre-conscious condition; if in some cases the ego definitely decides to bear this sort of burden in a future incarnation—how can we reconcile this belief (or truth) with the various methods of healing now outlined? For if certain souls destined to suffer cannot escape from suffering, how is it that the people in the spirit world are allowed to give information which will cure disease?

We answer that truly there is a law of redemption by suffering. But as the man evolves and becomes more conscious spiritually, the cruder conditions of the outworking of sin through so stern a discipline can be transmuted. Man may eradicate his past and rebuild his future by the higher and finer discipline of spiritual conquest over his baser self.

Sometimes we are able to watch a spiritual healer at work on his patient. The patient fails to respond, so the treatment seems futile. In some of these cases even the Great Ones who hold humanity in their care do not interfere, knowing that only by its own effort and striving, by attainment of mastery over itself can the soul transmute its own dark inheritance. Let us remember that Jesus Christ said to such a sinner, ' Thy sins are forgiven thee; go and sin no more.' The power and presence of Christ can accomplish even this if the erring soul will only seek to gain Him through victory over itself.

All diseases can be healed, and will some day be eradicated when the mass of humanity, of its own freewill and accord, comes to the temple of the living God to receive that pure white light, that truth, that living love, which flows from the heart of the Eternal, and is the very water of life. Then there will be no more weeping and wailing, but only man perfected.

As real happiness can only be earned, so also must perfect health and harmony between all of man's bodies be earned. No man need trail through fires of suffering to learn of God. Man can find God more readily through peace of heart, through joy. This is rather an ultimate path Godward, for man must first learn self-denial, self-conquest. But the way lies open. Here again we touch on good and evil, positive and negative, pain and joy. Man can settle with himself to go either way, to take the left or the right hand path. He can return to the Father either by his own aspiration or through some form of transmutation of his sin. The arms of the Father are ever open and waiting for His son.

We have said that all humanity can be grouped into the four divisions of Fire, Air, Earth and Water. The horoscope will enable the healer to place his patients correctly. He might, of course, allocate them by intuition or sensing, but the more scientific method is to cast the horoscope, thereby finding the exact ray of birth. Some months ago you received a description of the rays under which I myself was born. This unusual combination has caused me difficulty both during my life and immediately following death, as you will remember.

We could almost say that all disease is fundamentally caused by broken rhythm, by broken vibrations. The twelve rays hold humanity as it were in a grip of iron. In them lies the secret of man's well-being. When more is known of them, life will be simplified; much of its strain and stress will disappear, as well as obscure diseases which baffle medical science. They are due to man's inharmonic relationship to the magnetic forces and universal powers in which he has his being.

Some people may jeer at this, saying, ' Nonsense, we understand and know how to treat the body perfectly well.' My friends, you do not; you have not even begun to understand the physical body of man. Medical science must go farther afield, open wider its gates. Certainly surgery has become a fine art from which remarkable cures are resulting; and for accidents which cause torn and broken bodies surgery has its place. Even so surgery will some day be supplanted.

So far we have dealt with diseases common to all humanity, with the exception of those classified as infectious. It must seem confusing, in view of what we have said about the pre-conscious origin of many diseases, to find that infection can spread like wildfire through a community without apparent cause or reason. Yet numbers of people prove immune to it. Among these will be those who practise Christian Science, thus demonstrating that man's conscious mind holds a measure of control in these matters.

The Christian Scientist protects himself not only through mental action, but mainly because he has arrived at a point in his evolution when the need for this particular form of experience has been erased. We suggest that people who are subject to contagious diseases are ripe for the experience, and have a lesson to learn thereby.

With this few will agree, and will ask why little children should become infected. Should not their innocence protect them? To disclose the underlying cause of any physical disease we must cover a wide area; and we again suggest that the child comes prepared to undergo certain experiences which may take form as illness or suffering, or as health and happiness, and all the various fluctuations which go to mould human life and character. But contagion is not a necessary evil. In course of time, when spiritual laws are better understood, infection will go. Nor need anyone suffer now if he knows how to protect himself. The cell-life of the body, which is controlled by both the conscious and subconscious minds, can be held responsible for these invasions. If there is sufficient resistance by healthy conscious and subconscious thought-action, the cells of the body will repel the enemy. Therefore a child should be trained in right thinking from the first. The child's education should begin not at the age of seven or so, but from birth. Parents and nurse must realise that an infant absorbs thought either good or harmful into its very being from the atmosphere, from its environment, from the aura of parent, nurse, relatives and friends. A child fed with *positive thought* is fed with the breath of health, and will thrive physically, mentally and spiritually, and resist ill from every source.

These truths of child health and welfare will gradually dawn. At no distant date the human family must realise its responsibility towards the young souls entrusted to its care, and through this realisation awake to the responsibility it bears to the whole community.

WE have spoken of the broken rhythm or vibrations of man's physical body, which can cause a premature death. You may also apply this same law of broken rhythm to the human family, to man both individual and collective, and to the world as a whole. Let us pause to reflect, for this is vastly important. Must not this broken rhythm or harmony bring out a mind disease, a moral infection, which can affect nations and the well-being of a whole world?

It must be so. It is already happening. The world is sickening almost unto death in this year of 1932. We might despair did we not know of the great spiritual powers which can yet save mankind, if man will be saved. What is most needed now is the healing of all peoples, the healing of the nations. Pray God that it may come about.

CHAPTER X

THE HEALING OF THE NATIONS

'*O Thou Who art the Author of all good things; Thou Who art ever present, ever loving, wise and all powerful; we would come into Thy Presence. May the rays from Thy being permeate our very souls. May the light of Thy beauty illumine our minds, and may the power of Thy greatness enfold us in loving arms, so that we become one with Thee.*

Bless this work; may no shadow of doubt or fear fall across the light which Thou hast ordained shall come to the people of the earth. Amen.'

WE would emphasise again and yet again the need for a common brotherhood among men and nations. For only when humanity as a whole quickens, realises and understands that the whole race lives, moves, and has its being in a universal spiritual Force which continually sustains everything, can it save itself from eventual destruction. Let us not lose hope; it is indeed true that the values of life will some day be entirely changed. Would that conditions would change with them; for man will be forced through the sheer suffering and privation he will presently undergo to seek this greater truth to sustain him.

How simple it would seem to tell men about this truth, which is everywhere and in everything. But what a complicated conundrum it is for the worldly-minded! Yet over here in the spirit land all souls are brought at last to this understanding, and are only too thankful to believe, share and live safe within the fold of universal brotherhood.

No other way of living is open to the world. At present the nations subsist on suspicion and fear. None will give way, for each is afraid of the other. In the business world nearly every man is fighting against his fellow to secure and hold to himself his own particular grain of corn. Whither is all this leading man? Most surely neither to security nor to enduring prosperity, but to the fast tearing down of all that civilisation has laboriously established.

LET us take heart; in days to come we shall see humanity ennobled. There will presently dawn a vision of true brotherhood to uplift man's heart. He will then know that all life— his own and that of everyone else—is contained within one stupendous Heart of Love; and he will recognise that even his physical life pulses with its beating. He will know that he cannot hurt his brother without suffering a corresponding injury himself; for to hate or go to war with any man or nation is to go to war with himself. To slay another man is spiritual death to the slayer. That is why it is said that those who draw the sword must surely perish by the sword.

The new man to come will know that he can draw no breath, think no thought, without reaction throughout the world. He will know that death can never ultimately reign in God's Universe; that when man once understands himself and God, neither heaven nor earth can hold aught for him of death. For the new man there can be neither beginning nor ending, for he will see life as one unending Cycle, ever evolving, ever revolving, which holds every human soul in its embrace for evermore. If he violates one law, one truth of God, he must affect the well-being of all men. It is true; adversity must bind the soul of man to its fellow ere the world shall find such salvation as this. We are witnessing on your earth today the havoc wrought by materialism. This is death; death through materialism; and incidentally, the beginning of *death to materialism.**

Materialism will die hard; hence the suffering which must come. How else can it be when man has worshipped Mammon so often and so long? After sore pangs of suffering we see a

---

* It should be remembered that these words were spoken in 1932, in an age of selfish materialism which ushered in the Second World War.

new birth, the dawning of a new, a glorious Day of spiritual realisation, spiritual recognition. A spiritual basis for man's communal life will come. In every art and culture, in science, statecraft, and religion, man will be inspired and directed from the Halls of Wisdom.

MUCH more can be said about this universal brotherhood of which we tell. Alas, few men understand the meaning of the word; for most men have been taught from childhood to fight for themselves, to assert themselves at the expense of others even if they destroy their neighbour. Man has erroneously believed that the whole object of life is the enhancement of his personal self. At all costs he must become a man superior to others if he desires to be a master of life and of his brother man. This way of living sins against the cosmic law of brotherhood at every turn. A man who seeks to gain only for himself breaks every spiritual law; and while collective man continues to do the same the result can only be diseased bodies and minds, chaos and war.

The truly great man is he who submits to the infinite and eternal power of love in place of his own desires. Each soul must lose itself in order to find itself. No man will ever discover God while under the error that his power and his accomplishments come about by and through himself. The soul when it has arisen and thrown off the grave clothes of its egotism must pass a supreme test, and let all sense of self fall away. It must then face an abyss of blackness and seeming extinction. One desire only must sustain that fainting soul—to yield, to surrender, to be deprived utterly, to sacrifice every vestige of self so that it can merge into the infinite and eternal love which is God.

Surrender such as this is never extinction; it is expansion. For when a man reaches that point when his love of God becomes so overwhelming that he desires only to identify himself with God, then his love can draw God to him and enfold even the Deity; then every man will seem godlike to him because he sees God dwelling in all.

The man who would understand universal brotherhood must

indeed ' leave all and follow Me '. He must render up, must efface himself, must lose self in order to find the universal selflessness which is God. In this supreme moment the man becomes at-one not only with God, but with himself and with each and every creature. This is atonement, at-one-ment with God.

This is the meaning of the Brotherhood of Man.

MAN's bitter travail, his evolution, his progress, will bring him some day to such an end as this; he strives ever forward to the time when there will be but one brotherly thought prevailing, one pure harmony, one selfless desire and pure love abroad in the world. Never, never will man become established in aught but his own sorrow so long as he seeks for personal gain or supremacy.

Only one true religion exists, only one Reality behind all form, belief, sect, creed and ceremony. This is a universal religion, neither bound nor circumscribed by geographical limitations, convention or prejudice. It has but one name. That name can be understood by any and every man, white, black, yellow or red; by every woman and child; by animal and by bird, by tree and flower, and every creature instinct with the breath of life. The religion of true brotherhood has but one meaning and one name, and that is Love.

LOVE such as this must surely come; and love will teach men that forms and ceremonies, creeds and dogmas avail nothing without the living spirit. Every living creature can bear witness and respond to spiritual power. Man has racial diversities and many a diverse belief. Let each man have his due. But all must ultimately recognise and bow to the infinite love of the Creator. Then at last will man learn that he who works for all men works for God.

Not until that great day will the earth be wholly freed from death. Yes, with the dawning of that day when all men live in harmony, bowing their will to yet worshipping the supreme Law, death will indeed be swallowed up in victory.

Then the flesh of man will yield no longer to the overlordship of death, for it will be transmuted. Sin in very truth is death; death, the result of sin. We mean that exactly as it is said. Sin will assuredly bring death in some form; but love, wise, pure and true, will give eternal life.

Every word uttered by the great Master rings with truth, a truth unsullied by passing time, eternal and absolute.

PART III

RETROSPECT

RETROSPECT

I

SUCH was the Message. We have omitted many a piece of circumstantial evidence given in *Thy Kingdom Come*, where Conan Doyle spoke intimately to his family of their private affairs subsequent to his death; where he showed to the group his knowledge of contemporary events in the Spiritualist movement and also of wider developments in world affairs—namely, of matters which had all occurred since his passing. Those who had known him personally—his family, Miss Estelle Stead, Mr. W. R. Bradbrook (the Secretary of the Memorial Fund)—realised by every trait of his personality, by his mannerisms, his old energy and masculinity, his sheer force of character and warm-hearted enthusiasm and affection—that this was the man, Arthur Conan Doyle, as he was in life, though with his character now more sublimated by his experiences. On the other hand the medium, her husband and friends, had never met Conan Doyle before his passing. The personality who spoke through the medium possessed a knowledge and power of expression, and a literary style quite foreign to the medium; and the change of semblance in the medium, both facial and in habits and gestures was remarked on by everyone present. Moreover, there was no question of telepathy; here was a man speaking in precise detail, and at the end of his discourses taking up and replying to any argument or query. Nor was there any question of it being the higher-self of the medium speaking and answering; the personality of A.C.D. was felt as strongly as was his presence, his character, and the spiritual power and upliftment that were given him to bring through his message. It was the sense of *life* that was so convincing—of free, untrammelled life, the marvellous potentialities and expansion of our sense of life beyond bodily limitation. This sense lifted the discourse above the ordinary mundane or mental level. Here was no phantasm, no ethereal and temporary projection of the mind from its inner recesses. Moreover, the work continued over a long period and the man was intensely alive and real throughout. In fact, his character was far stronger than that of any earthly person present, vibrant, forceful, integrated, yet wider in range of human understanding and sympathy. This was no longer the sick, worn-out and ageing Doyle who passed in 1930; but a man whose force and vitality impinged upon everyone present in the room.

What should we rightfully expect from the dead if they returned? Mere memories about their former life? We should surely expect, if they were still living, to hear something about their new experiences. If this man had formerly been competent, of fearless mind and upright character, disdaining all that he thought shallow or untruthful, then in his case an exact account of his experiences might reasonably be expected. If, moreover, during his life he held some misconceptions regarding life after death, would he not strive to put them right, particularly if they were of consequence to those people who had shared his former beliefs? Indeed, he would leave no stone unturned to give his new message. In fine, if the man lived, then his validity and character should survive death; for these, it is commonly said, are the only attributes a man is left with on his deathbed.

This then was the Doyle who came back, changed in some of his opinions, full of his new experiences, uplifted, and in every sense alive; yet still retaining the character known to all associated with him. To his family he remained still their father. But he wished and he was determined that his message should come through to the world at large. Furthermore, he intended his message to be self-evident.

For one cannot go into a court of law and say, ' I have irrefragable evidence that one Arthur Conan Doyle is still present and alive; here he is; let him go into the witness-box himself and give evidence.' Yet Conan Doyle, discarnate, put himself in the witness-box, not before a court but before the world at large—or at least before those who would pause to hear his testimony. He said, in other words, ' This is I, Conan Doyle; I cannot come to you in a material body such as yours, but yet

I can by certain means render my evidence. Let my evidence be recorded and read out. My affidavit is given in the presence of those who knew me, who would testify to my identity if I were in a material body. I give you a proof cogent and reasonable. And if it is I—then with a fair and open mind listen to my testimony.

'This very testimony that the dead live and therefore have identity, naturally I could not give while I was in a material body. But now I have made it circumstantial. If it be the work of a forger or imitator, judge for yourselves. On the other hand, if it does not conform with people's views—or absence of views—on life after death, or their religious preconceptions, you cannot expect me to offer as my sole evidence an array of facts which were already known to me and others during my life-time. There must indeed be something new if I have gained in experience. And yet any novelty that I bring can be seen in perspective, if you will study the scriptures of world religions, and the writings of the mystics;* or if you will open yourselves to the realisation that God is a God of Love, and that there is harmony, order and reasonableness throughout the universe. Then you will see that the progression of man through death to the after-life is based on a man's own nature and deserts; that his after-state is the logical outcome of his own growth and expansion, and the development of the life within him. Finally, that after death you live still in a rational and not a fanciful universe, where facts are yet facts.'

A FURTHER matter of considerable interest was the evidence given to a representative from the Polaires in Paris. White Eagle dictated certain figures in a cipher which was able to be comprehended by the Polaires alone. This, in itself, constituted an objective and mathematical proof of the veracity of his statements, and one notable in the whole range and history of Spiritualism.

---

* The 'sayings' of the Wise Men of past ages which head many chapters in the book confirm this statement.

In addition to this proof there are other considerations. The Polaires—it will be remembered from Part I—obtained their knowledge of the Wise Knight and his brethren—together with their directions to take part in the reception of the messages from Conan Doyle—by one means alone, the Oracle de Force Astrale, which operated solely through a series of numbers translatable in strict accordance with an arithmetical key. When a question had been transmitted, the answer resolved itself into a *series of digits*, which were then translatable into perfectly spelt words. These words were, however, still in an incomprehensible order, and it required a further calculation by the operator to place them, however numerous, in correct sequence. The result was now an intelligible message.

Both question and answer had perforce to be in Italian, for the key was for that language alone. The Polaires themselves did not possess this key, which remained throughout with the original possessor who kept its secret undivulged.

The Polaires, who had received through the oracle in November 1930 precise directions concerning the messages about to be given by Conan Doyle, now required proof that White Eagle had access to the spiritual chiefs who directed the Polaire brotherhood, and that his words concerning Conan Doyle were valid. This proof he gave first by a brief description of their leader in chief, then by describing a vision the import of which was plain to the Polaires, and finally by dictating a *series of digits*, the reason for which was comprehensible to the Polaires and to no one else present.

First, as has been said, this cipher was in itself a remarkable piece of cross-evidence, for numbers, unlike words, to mean anything must be all of them exact.

Secondly, as we have shown, the code which gave—to quote the words of the Polaires—a ' *very precise* check ' was almost certainly that of the Oracle de Force Astrale, in which the answers given by the Sages formed in the first place a series of digits. As White Eagle was himself, it was afterwards disclosed, a Tibetan Sage, the hypothesis is not unrealistic.

As a counter-check, it may be added, the Polaires sealed and deposited with a Paris notary the communications regarding this very sitting which they had themselves received through the oracle. Having obtained the necessary proof, they published the results of the sitting in their magazine—from which the following extracts are taken.*

(*White Eagle is speaking of the spiritual leaders of the Polaire movement, and of their chief, the Wise Knight, the Knight of the Rose-Cross:*)

' The Great Beings are near me. Now White Eagle is in contact with the Chevalier Sage. What a marvellous being! White Eagle perceives his great black eyes and his white robe decorated with a red cross. It is He who directs the Polaire movement. It is He who projects Love and Brotherhood upon the world.

' . . . Now I must describe to you a vision. I have to indicate to you the numbers 3 and 9, which are of very great importance: $3 \times 3 = 9$. There is the entrance to a cavern. On the dark rocks shines the six-pointed star. On the floor a sword in its scabbard. A serpent entwined about a staff. The creature speaks: *Man has descended through his own selfwill into the mire. He has now to break loose from his circle of sorrow and darkness. Of his own freewill he ' lost' his paradise, and he will not regain it save by his own will and by an immense effort.*

' . . . My Brother, you know the reason why White Eagle should dictate to you certain numbers? This is no easy thing, but I will do my best to communicate those which I see inscribed for you. I must make them known for a purpose which only you will understand. Then write XXV, now XV, next IV, and then III. Write down V and II, afterwards C and LV. Finally a V and a I.'

Regarding these numbers, ' B.Z.' (that is, Zam Bhotiva)

---

* *Bulletin des Polaires*, Paris, issue of March 9th, 1931, from which these extracts are a literal translation. The person addressed as ' my Brother' was M. Bhotiva, who again as representative of the Polaire Brotherhood in Paris had come to this sitting held at Wembley Park, Middlesex, on March 3rd, 1931—the third sitting at which the Polaires were represented. The details of the numerical code are taken from M. Bhotiva's book, *Asia Mysteriosa*, Paris, 1929, pages 38-40.

added the following notes. Of the 3 × 3 = 9: ' *These numbers relate to the series of digits in Roman numerals given later.*' And of the series of Roman numerals themselves: ' *These digits were given for the purpose of a* VERY PRECISE *check, which has enabled us to take account of the source of these communications.*'

The message concealed under these Roman numerals was not made public, but this much may be disclosed—that White Eagle was working from the same centre as the Chevalier Sage, in close co-operation and complete harmony (as they work still); and the proof that this was so lay in the particular numerals given to M. Bhotiva.

THESE considerations regarding the authenticity of the Message merit further respect because of the reception accorded to *Thy Kingdom Come* at its publication. It found the bulk of its readers, not among the Spiritualists (as might be expected) but among the general public. Spiritualism as a whole is apt to term anything outside survivalism ' Theosophic,' while the Theosophist calls anything of which he disapproves ' Spiritualistic '; which is a pity, because Spiritualism could have made Theosophy more human and Theosophy made Spiritualism more thoughtful.

Surprisingly, the book interested both the Theosophist and the occultist. A leading occultist hailed it as the best and most accurate description of the Life-after-Death he had met. A number both of occult groups and Theosophical Lodges held a series of lectures based on *Thy Kingdom Come*; which was also read widely by the general public, the leading lending libraries having it on their booklists. When it went out-of-print shortly after the outbreak of the recent war there was a keen demand for secondhand copies, which has continued ever since. Everywhere it has won a quiet acceptance as being true.

THE writer believes that the latter part of Chapter I in Part II deserves special study, for in it A.C.D. gives the key to the nature of the next world. That key is the word ' externalisation '; for here and now we are continually externalising ourselves in all that we do and are, and do so from infancy onwards. The result is that our homes and families, our hobbies and habits, our trades or businesses are all exact expressions of ourselves; as are our face and its expression, our state of health, our body, its gait and bearing, our habits of thought, our speech and mannerisms. All proclaim exactly what we are because they are externalisations of our real or inner self. This may be a truism, but is one often overlooked. What few of us realise, however, is that with the same unfailing accuracy we are externalising ourselves on the invisible world around us. By so doing we are preparing both the condition and environment to which we shall go after death, and this by a process which might almost be called automatic. Truly, man makes his own heaven. He also makes an alternative place, if he so wills.

Secondly, what is the key which opens up contact with the next world? It is Love. By Love is meant loving-kindness not only to a few people, but as a habitual expression of ourselves to all living creatures, to the world we live in, to life itself, and to God. Love such as this alone bridges the gulf between this world and the next, and itself governs the quality both of communication and communion with those in the life beyond. Those who seek contact with relatives ' over there ' through a medium will truly succeed only if they have loving hearts—if they are broad and big-hearted, warm, loving and wise in their loving. Then the gates are flung wide. So also with those who would so raise themselves that they may commune on the Plane of Reunion. Warm human love is the one factor which will raise them. No amount of mental strain or struggle will avail; for there love alone prevails.

' Externalisation ' then is the keyword which makes the rulings and conditions of the next life comprehensible. We externalise ourselves into that life. It in turn reflects back into our mortal lives while we are living here, so that we can always be in touch with more worlds than one. ' Love ' is the second keyword which ultimately means the difference between hell and heaven both in this life and the next. Although these matters are serious, we need not be too gloomy about them, because an element of mercy, of compassionate understanding, pervades all worlds. We can be far harder in our judgment of ourselves than God will ever be. But these two momentous words contain the essence of the A.C.D. message; and for this reason they are stressed.

II

THE publication of Conan Doyle's message in *Thy Kingdom Come* was, moreover, by no means the end of the story, but part of one much longer and no less significant. Its events, which can here only be summarised, began after the 'Two-Two Day' meeting on May 22nd, 1931, which was described in Part I. The cause was another message through the 'Oracle de Force Astrale.' The Polaires were told that a certain 'treasure' was concealed at a ruined castle in the French Pyrenees; for the lofty hill on which the castle stood had once been a sacred temple, a secret shrine of the Albigensian brotherhood. This treasure, whatever it might be, they were instructed to recover.

History has almost forgotten about the 'Albigenses,' a people, it is known, who came from the East and spread westward across Southern Europe early in the eleventh century. In the south of France they received the name of Albigenses. Though their origin still remains largely obscure, mystics believe that their original founder (though many centuries earlier) was John, to whom are attributed the Book of Revelation and the Fourth Gospel—the Gospel which mystics declare will be that of the New Age. The following account is quoted, partly summarised, from *The Return of the Magi* by Maurice Magre, who devoted many years' study to the history of the Albigenses.

'It was in the regions of Albi, Toulouse and Carcassonne that the mystical revolution took place. Afterwards, for nearly a century and a half the doctrine spread over the south of France and into Italy and Germany, where it found many adherents. Renunciation of material goods and possessions became a moral law which spread among its followers with astonishing rapidity. From Bordeaux to the borders of Provence, in stern Languedoc, under the chestnuts of the Albi district and on the moors of Lauragais, the roads were full of ascetics eager to tell their brothers what the spirit had revealed to them. It was always the humble in spirit who received this inspiration. Nor was it confined to the layman. In the poplar avenue and the stone cloister where walked a hundred shaven-headed monks it breathed sometimes with such contagious power that it caused the gates to be shut and the garden and chapel to be abandoned. Estranged more and more from the God of the churches, the God of rich prelates and pitiless barons, the followers of the Albigenses worshipped the inner God whose light grew ever brighter the purer their own lives became, the more they became charged with love for their fellow men.'

Within the sect were distinct grades. There were the ordinary adherents, among whom many of the nobility of the south of France were numbered; these corresponded to those who followed the 'Middle Path' recommended by Buddhism for the majority of men; and there were the *perfecti*, or the adepts, who sacrificed all ease and comfort of body for the spirit.

Through the *consolamentum*, the adepts had power to open an approach to the heavenly worlds; for these adepts were heirs to a lost secret, a secret which had come from the East and was known to the gnostics and the early Christians. It should be understood that while St. Paul had provided a basis for, and even founded the Christian Church for the masses, some mystics believe that an inner group or brotherhood was also established by Jesus Christ, the leader of which was John, called the Beloved of his Master. He it was who had first been entrusted with the *consolamentum*, the secret of which was the transmission of the supreme power of love, the rite itself being the material and visible means of projecting this power. Behind it was hidden the spiritual gift by which the soul of the dying was helped, was able to cross without suffering the gulf of death, to escape the shadowy astral lands and merge into the light.

'Never has any people at any period been so deeply versed in magical rites concerning death,' the author continues. 'The *consolamentum* must have possessed a power which to present-day people is quite inconceivable . . . the inspiration of the dying must have been actually visible to the onlookers, for the adepts had knowledge which today is lost . . .'

In other words, the true cult of the Albigenses had been that of the Holy Spirit, the divine Paraclete—that is to say, of the *principle* which enables the human spirit to attain to the real world (of which this world is but the reverse side, the shadow) —the world of pure light, the ' permanent and unalterable City.'

For nearly 200 years the Albigenses gained in numbers, but the end of their movement was tragic indeed. A campaign was launched by the Church of Rome early in the thirteenth century, aided by the king and armies of the north of France, together with mercenaries from other lands. Adherents and adepts alike, all must die, for all were heretics. Hundreds of the ' heretics ' were walled up in caves to die of hunger and cold, were thrown into the flames, or cast from mountain heights into chasms below. Man, woman and child, they each met savage deaths, mostly without flinching and in a spirit of calm heroism. Not even the bodies of those who had previously died naturally could escape desecration; they were dug up and maltreated. And after it was all over—after twenty years of bloodshed— even the few children of the ' heretics ' who remained alive were cast out and so clothed that men might know of their parents' shame. In all, this is known as the greatest and cruellest massacre of mediaeval times.

It is said that none of the adepts escaped, but certainly some of the adherents did, for again and again something of the faith and freedom of thought brought by the original brothers from the East manifested, and was again and again savagely suppressed and thought to be exterminated by further massacres and by the Holy Inquisition. Some think that Protestantism itself had its beginning with the advent of the Albigenses. This is as may be. What is quite certain is that no religion of past or present, the Christianity of Paul not excluded, has ever brought such tidings or such consolation to mankind about death and its aftermath as did the revelation of the Albigenses. Neither Spiritualism nor occultism have any such contribution to make;

for it is said that even those Albigenses who were walled up to die in caves or flung into the flames saw heaven itself revealed and were caught up in its glory.

Nor must it be supposed that those who killed the adepts had any power over their souls—especially these illumined souls. During mortal life they were pent up within their personal selves. Afterwards they were freed, each in his degree (as was Jesus set free) to serve in a more subtle manner, but more widely.

So the souls of these adepts should be thought of as intensely alive, albeit invisible, exerting an influence which can still be felt within the mountain lands they once inhabited. They bless them still with their unseen presence; the passage of years means little or nothing to them; despite the centuries their influence still reaches mankind. They watch, for they have still power to assist men as the occasion arises. Such an occasion was undoubtedly the coming through of the A.C.D. message. The invisible powers ever work in conjunction; and theirs may have been the inspiration behind the original instructions which came through the Force Astrale. They may have worked in conjunction with the Wise Knight—the Knight of the Rose-Cross. Certainly the complete A.C.D. message might be considered as something akin to the *consolamentum*, and as preparing the way for it someday to be restored to men.

If this be accepted, then it is indeed natural and reasonable that they should send for Minesta, that she should be brought to that particular mountain on which had been their shrine, and there be blessed, there initiated into the lesser mysteries, in order that the knowledge and power thus imparted might facilitate the coming through of A.C.D.'s message concerning the heavenly life.

Because of her belief in the Sages, Minesta journeyed to this hill, which was over 3,000 feet high, rising above a deep valley, and ringed about with greater heights which were still snow-capped in summer. Once among the ruins of the castle on the crest of the hill, she felt that she must isolate herself from the rest of the party. They were hurried, over-eager to find the treasure. By now she was not convinced that any material treasure existed. Day after day while the party pursued the search, Minesta became more aware of the presence and reality of the unseen Brethren on that height. Many of the Albigenses had perished there. Human bones were found here and there only a foot or so beneath the surface of the ground.

But the *perfecti* or adepts still watched over their shrine. They came close and spoke to the soul of Minesta, telling her whence they had come and what had been the faith for which they had died. It was true—John the Beloved had been their Master— John of the Fourth Gospel—John who had been entrusted with the gnostic wisdom, and bidden to found an inner, mystical Brotherhood or Church of Christ, much as St. Paul had been called to establish the outer Church of Peter. During the centuries to come, the message of John would enter and inspire the hearts of men. The secret of all secrets which was theirs had been the *consolamentum* for the dying, which alone had power to lift men literally from earth to heaven by unveiling heaven itself before them; and this even by a word, a glance, a touch of the hand from an adept. Yet not in words alone could that secret be imparted—perhaps it could never be written down in words. Power to impart that secret could only be gained by living the life of renunciation—such as had been their life.

In a measure, they told her, they had entrusted their secret to her soul. She must go from there preserving it secure. Hers had been a minor initiation into their mysteries. It remained to see what use she might make of it in the modern world. She had in fact been called and initiated there because it would help the A.C.D. message to come through with greater purity and force.

Meanwhile the rest of the party were busily delving into many places and finding many strange things, but not a treasure either material or otherwise. The time came for Minesta to return home. Ostensibly the expedition had failed. Yet had it failed? The Oracle de Force Astrale had only promised that Minesta should find the treasure. No mention had been made of others. What had she brought away as the result of her visit?

Succeeding years were to prove. We mortals are apt to think

that we ourselves decide our every course of action. This may be so on occasion. Mostly, it would seem, in every important action we are *impelled* to do this or that. Most certainly it was so with Minesta during the years which followed. In the first place she had felt impelled to undertake the work for A.C.D. Then she felt she was bidden to go to the castle where difficulties and dangers abounded—for there were grave dangers there quite apart from those to life and limb. For long months after her return she laboured with A.C.D.'s message, now constrained to do so by an impulse she could not resist.

Shortly after the return from the Pyrenees, a branch of the Polaire Brotherhood was started in England under Minesta's leadership. Its title and method of working were subsequently changed, and it is now believed that these became more in accord with the ancient Albigensian methods. Two years later, with the publication of the book *Thy Kingdom Come*, a considerable problem arose.

Merely to publish the A.C.D. message was not enough, it was felt. For any book is soon forgotten. How could the A.C.D. message be kept alive? As with the messages of earlier teachers, there seemed only one way, which was to make it a basic faith for a community, and thereby to test it out to see whether it worked. This was done; under White Eagle's guidance a humble beginning was made at a small hall in West London, opened in 1936. It was named 'The White Eagle Lodge'— the word 'lodge' denoting a place where a 'family' might gather ; and the initiating and sustaining power behind the work was that of White Eagle, under whose guidance and with whose co-operation and assistance the A.C.D. message was given; and upon whose subsequent teaching the work has gone forward. Yet in those early days A.C.D.'s message was its foundation.

III

Since 1936 the White Eagle Lodge has grown far beyond anything dreamt of in those early days, and through many a ' miracle ' has proved again and again the guiding hand of the sages. When in 1940 the original premises were destroyed by a bomb, new premises, more suitable in every way for the ever expanding work, were soon found, and the work continues there to this day. Later, under White Eagle's guidance and instruction, a country centre for spiritual retreat and instruction was sought and found at New Lands in Hampshire. The London Lodge, New Lands, and the rapidly growing third branch of the work, the White Eagle Publications, all became registered as Charitable Religious Trusts, thus not only safeguarding the future of the work but also ensuring that no private profit could ever be made from it.

It was realised from the outset that with a horizon as wide as that opened up by the A.C.D. message many subjects were dealt with far too briefly and this has been rectified gradually by the publication of books of White Eagle's teaching which expand A.C.D's. original statements. Many thousands of ' White Eagle ' books are being despatched each year from New Lands, which has become the administrative centre for the work of the Lodge and Publishing Trust. There must be few, if any English speaking countries in the world where these books are not being read today, and it is felt that they carry an influence with them, a ray maybe, from the Chevalier Rose Croix or from the Brothers of the Mountain.

What started as a venture of faith has continued in faith until today its influence touches thousands of lives through its books and through the Lodges at London and New Lands and daughter lodges and small groups in many parts of the world.* Spiritual healing, originally based on the chapter on the ' Healing of all Disease ' in the A.C.D. message, has ever been an important aspect of the work of these Lodges and groups, and the White Eagle healers now treat hundreds of patients every year, with some outstanding results.

Establishing the fact of man's survival after death is a vital part of Arthur Conan Doyle's message, and so one asks, what has been done about this in the White Eagle Lodges? In the early

---

* Full details of all the White Eagle publications, records and cassettes can be obtained from the White Eagle Publishing Trust.

days of the Lodge individual proof of survival was given to numbers of people, especially to the recently bereaved; but as the years went by, it became clear that White Eagle and the brothers wished to help people to find their own contact with the world of spirit through meditation and spiritual communion. Now, individual messages are seldom given, but countless sad, bereaved people have found their own consolation and certain knowledge that their loved ones are still with them. This knowledge, which we can surely call the consolamentum, and the certainty that all life is one, is strong in the Lodge, strong in the lives of its members and friends and many who just read its books. It is now plain that Minesta was taken to the mountain top all those years ago to establish the link with the ancient consolamentum. This was the treasure she brought away.

There has been a perfect plan behind all that has happened—behind the bestowal of the Force Astrale, the formation of the Polaire Group, their linking with Arthur Conan Doyle, his message through Minesta, and the founding of the Lodge. In 1966 another stage of the plan was revealed. The sages directed that a White Temple should be built on the hill top by New Lands, and that this Temple was to be the focal point, from which the spiritual light and teaching, the spiritual treasure of the consolamentum, was to be given to the world. The White Temple was eventually built and opened to the public on 9th June 1974, but preparations for this, (although unknown to anyone on earth) began many years before. In 1956 Minesta again visited the Pyrenees, impelled by a hidden spiritual purpose.

Again she climbed to the crest of the hill—almost a small mountain in itself—and found the shrine of the adepts, despite other changes in the neighbourhood, as remote and isolated as before. There were still traces of the excavations by the Polaires twenty-five years earlier, but all sense of their restlessness and haste had departed, leaving the place entirely peaceful. As before, the Brethren were waiting for her, seemingly as real—more real—to Minesta's trained vision than would have been mortals standing at her side.

They spoke with her, and through her to a group of brothers

who had accompanied her, saying that in the mountains around were certain air currents which made it easier for the cosmic rays to penetrate, and that the pure and holy devas who guard those heights also watch over human evolution. They said that humanity as a whole was about to rise to a higher level of life. Therefore the watchers from the heavens were on the alert. It was also literally true that St. John the Beloved had once come to this holy place on the heights. This was the source of its ancient power which had kept the Albigenses loyal even to death; the source of the consolamentum, the 'consoling', which could overcome the dark veil between the physical and heavenly worlds.

Knowledge and power to use this consolamentum had long been the desire of men, who searched for it and called it by various names; it was part of the mystic's attainment of the 'holy grail'; it was the 'lost word' for want of which Freemasonry languished. But it could only be imparted to those who lived in purity and truth; all others would be blind and deaf to its significance.

These brothers of an older time had watched over the delivery of A.C.D.'s message and its outcome in London. They saw the effect of that work as a great etheric building already taking shape in the world invisible which interpenetrated this world. They had constantly held that work within their ray of love and compassion, which took away the fear of death from those who could respond to it.

During the great massacre of the Albigenses, their enemies had power only to kill men's bodies. Sometimes this had set souls free to inherit a greater power, a more vigorous life; and this power they retained for service even in the world today. They had been able to sustain Minesta in the same way that they were behind every true and dedicated brother of these or earlier times.

Much more was said but these words epitomise the message. Minesta came away exalted by the wonder of this experience; and yet it was but a preparation for what was to come. For in 1966, when in Italy,* in a simple chapel of what was once a monastery the contact was again made with the sages and the plan for the building of the Temple was revealed. The ' etheric building ' described by the Brothers in 1956 was to take physical form; and so it did, as already described, in the summer of 1974.

It is difficult to compress any account of the history of the Lodge into a few pages, but at least this brief synopsis helps to demonstrate that the tangible proof promised by A.C.D. at the end of his message has indeed been given. The A.C.D. message has proved itself and continues to do so with every passing year. Every patient healed is a living testimony to the scheme of healing he set out; every person who finds that A.C.D's message provides a good working philosophy of life, a practical and hardworking religion which answers his questions and resolves his doubts, by so doing testifies to its truth. The existence of the Lodge, its expansion and the birth of many daughter groups, and then the building of the White Temple—these are all the promised tangible proofs.

The White Temple, its design a subtle blend of classical and modern architecture, a symbol of the ancient wisdom restated for the new age, is surely a fitting memorial to the spiritual work of Arthur Conan Doyle. The Conan Doyle message laid the foundation stone upon which the White Eagle Lodge and teaching has been built. As the light is sent forth daily (its focal point, the Temple), in prayer, meditation, healing of individuals, nations and the world, so his message lives on; and it may be that in time to come men will look back on this message and deem it the greatest and most significant among the works of Arthur Conan Doyle.

---

* The full account of this stage of the story is told in the booklet THE TEMPLE ANGEL, White Eagle Publishing Trust.

INDEX